DOLLS' CLOTHES PATTERN BOOK

Roselyn Gadia-Smitley

Sterling Publishing Co., Inc.   New York

Dolls shown in Color Section

Page A.   From top, clockwise: Barbie, Spanish Barbie, P.J., Malibu Christie, Spanish Barbie. All by Mattel, Inc.

Page B.   From left to right: Malibu Christie by Mattel, Inc.; Candi by Mego Corporation; Bride by Furga; Barbie by Mattel, Inc.

Page C.   Dolls on left and right: Chrissy and Turn Around Chrissy. Both by Ideal Toy Corporation. Doll in center: Dollikins by Uneeda.

Page D.   From left to right: P.J., Malibu Christie and Barbie. All by Mattel, Inc.

Page E.   From left to right: Baby Softskin by E. I. Horsman, Inc.; Starlet, unmarked doll used by Lustre Creme Shampoo for promotional purposes; Cabbage Patch Kid by Coleco Industries, Inc.

Pages F   All four dolls are Cabbage Patch Kids by Coleco Industries, Inc.
  and G.

Page H.   Doll on left is Cabbage Patch Kid by Coleco Industries, Inc.; small doll in front is unknown but by E. I. Horsman, Inc.; standing doll is unknown and unmarked.

Edited by Barbara Busch

Library of Congress Cataloging-in-Publication Data

Gadia-Smitley, Roselyn.
  Dolls' clothes pattern book.

  Includes index.
  1. Doll clothes—Patterns.   I. Title.
TT175.7.G33 1987   745.592′21   87-14369
ISBN 0-8069-6436-7
ISBN 0-8069-6438-3 (pbk.)

  5   7   9   10   8   6

Copyright © 1987 by Roselyn Gadia-Smitley
Published by Sterling Publishing Co., Inc.
Two Park Avenue, New York, N.Y. 10016
Distributed in Canada by Oak Tree Press Ltd.
% Canadian Manda Group, P.O. Box 920, Station U
Toronto, Ontario, Canada M8Z 5P9
Distributed in the United Kingdom by Blandford Press
Link House, West Street, Poole, Dorset BH15 1LL, England
Distributed in Australia by Capricorn Ltd.
P.O. Box 665, Lane Cove, NSW 2066
Manufactured in the United States of America
All rights reserved

CONTENTS

INTRODUCTION

t is not only fun but satisfying to make clothes for a doll. Whether you are sewing for a child or your very own doll collection, you can create an endless variety of styles based on the patterns of this book.

Basic understanding of sewing techniques is all that is needed for the completion of the projects. Leftover bits and pieces from other projects can be easily incorporated into a doll dress, which will provide an extensive wardrobe for the doll. Matching dresses have proven to be popular among children. Sewing doll clothes with the help of the child also provides learning as well as entertainment.

For the doll collector, it is very difficult to find the right type of clothing for a particular doll. This often leads to customizing a doll dress. Dress material can be obtained from old clothing which may come from one's wardrobe, antique shops, flea markets and other sources. It is advisable to research clothing made from the era of the doll. A doll's dress often reflects the clothing worn at the period it was made. Careful research in your local library will lead you to the type of clothing worn by the doll.

Sewing for a child's doll or for a collection has its rewards. For the doll collector, the original investment rises in value in addition to the enjoyment of the doll. For the child, doll clothes provide endless entertainment. For the seamstress, making doll clothing is both an act of giving as well as a creative expression.

HOW TO USE THIS BOOK

lothing for children has changed very little since the 1930's. Doll clothing reflects these clothing styles. With this information on hand, the author selected basic styles of clothing, representative of the doll frame: the Baby-Type Doll, Toddler-Type Doll, Girl-Type Doll, Teen-Type Doll, and the Lady-Type Doll. When data are available for a specific doll type, the author has striven to replicate the clothing worn by the doll at the time of its creation. To preserve a doll's hair, the author recommends placement of a bonnet or a hat on a doll's head.

Clothing patterns in this book are full-scale. Addition of trims, such as ribbons and laces, is optional.

Pattern Symbols

Pattern symbols are explained as follows:

↕   *Place the pattern parallel to the finished edge of the fabric (selvage).*

CF   *Means the center of the front of the pattern (Illus. 1).*

CB   *Means the center of the back of the pattern (Illus. 2).*

‖
or   *Lengthen or shorten in this section of the*
___   *pattern as needed.*

]   *Place the pattern on the fold of the fabric (Illus. 3).*

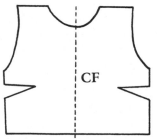

Illus. 1.   Center front of the pattern.

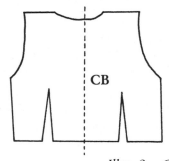

Illus. 2.   Center back of the pattern.

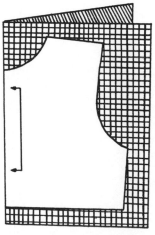

Illus. 3.   Placing the pattern on the fold of the fabric.

Increasing or Decreasing Patterns

Patterns may need to be increased or decreased, depending on the size of the doll (Illus. 4). To increase, simply spread out the cut pattern pieces (Illus. 5). Connect the gap with lines. To decrease, overlap the cut pattern pieces and redraw the lines. Transparent tape will hold the pattern pieces securely while you redraw the lines of the pattern. Repeat the same procedures to decrease or increase sleeves, skirts or pants (Illus. 6–9).

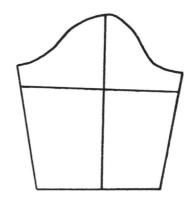

Illus. 7.   Intersecting lines for sleeves. Lines on sleeves should be drawn as illustrated.

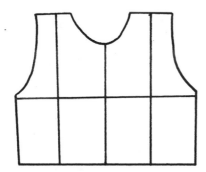

Illus. 4.   Marking the basic pattern. The primary step in increasing or decreasing the pattern is drawing the intersecting lines on the pattern. Mark the desired areas to be increased or decreased.

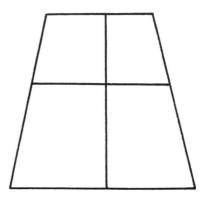

Illus. 8.   Intersecting lines for skirt. Lines on skirt should be drawn as illustrated.

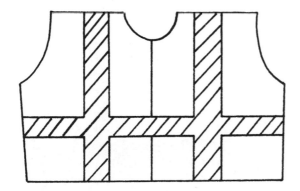

Illus. 5.   Increasing the pattern. By spreading apart the pattern pieces, the pattern size is increased. Redraw lines to connect the separate pieces.

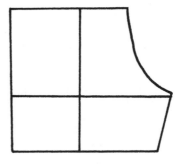

Illus. 9.   Intersecting lines for pants. Lines on pants should be drawn as illustrated.

Tips for Sewing

Fabric selection for doll clothing often dictates the degree of difficulty in the construction process. Choose fabrics which are easy to manage in the sewing machine, such as medium-weight cottons, medium-weight acetates and other stiffer fabrics. If a lightweight material is chosen, such as chiffon, tulle or voile, line the garment. This will stabilize the material. Basting, however, may be a necessity.

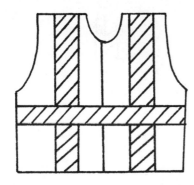

Illus. 6.   Decreasing the pattern. To decrease, overlap cut parts. Redraw lines to connect the separate pieces.

Due to the size of the clothing pieces, the feed dog of the sewing machine may tend to pull the fabric into the bobbin area, thus jamming the sewing machine. To prevent this from happening, gently pull the fabric along while sewing.

Assembling sections in units (*example:* joining parts of the front to form the front bodice, back, etc.) will add greatly to the organization and ease in the assembly of the doll clothing. Review I!lus. 10, 11, 12, 13, 14, 15, 16 and 17.

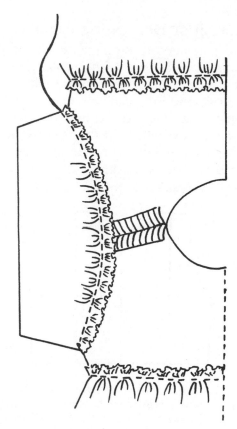

Illus. 12.   Attaching the sleeves. Sew the sleeves to the bodice before any further construction.

Illus. 10.   Assembling the front bodice of the doll clothing.

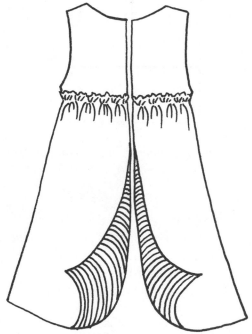

Illus. 11.   Assembling the back-bodice sections of the doll clothing.

Illus. 13.   Joining front- and back-bodice sections. After the sleeves are sewn to the bodice, close the side seams, starting from the hem of the skirt to the hem of the sleeves, as illustrated.

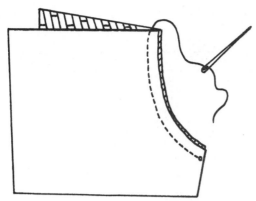

Illus. 14. *Sewing the crotch areas of the pants. Sewing two panels of pants will form the front or back sections of the pants.*

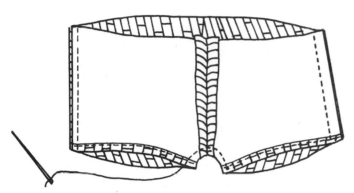

Illus. 15. *Closing the side seams and inner seams of the pants. Sewing the side seams, followed by closing the inner seams together, will greatly add to the ease of the construction process.*

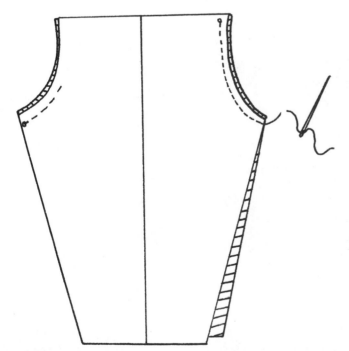

Illus. 16. *Sewing the crotch seams of a two-pant pattern.*

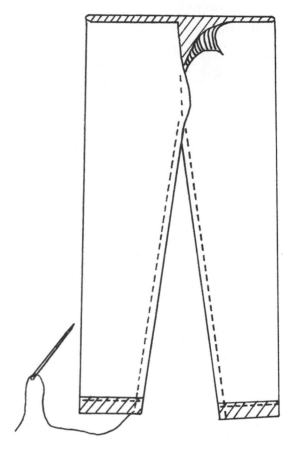

Illus. 17. *Hemming the pants and then closing the inner seams are steps that will greatly aid in the ease of the construction of the pants.*

Because of the small armholes, the most difficult part of sewing doll clothing is attaching the sleeves to the bodice. To sew the sleeves by machine, attach the sleeve cap to the bodice first. Proceed by closing the entire side of the garment, from sleeve to the hem of the dress, as shown in Illus. 13.

To ensure a perfect fit of the doll clothing, a paper dress or paper hat should be put together with transparent tape. Hats especially need this attention because doll-head sizes usually vary from one doll manufacturer to another.

Yardage Estimates

All yardage estimates on projects are based on a forty-five-inch fabric width.

The following yardage conversion chart is provided for your convenience:

For fabrics with naps or obvious one-direction prints, such as plaids and strips, add an additional one-quarter yard to your yardage estimate.

YARDAGE CONVERSION CHART

Fabric Width	35"–36"	44"–45"	50"	52"–54"	58"–60"
	1¾	1⅜	1¼	1⅛	1
	2	1⅝	1½	1⅜	1¼
	2¼	1¾	1⅝	1½	1⅜
Yardage	2½	2⅛	1¾	1¾	1⅝
	2⅞	2¼	2	1⅞	1¾
	3⅛	2½	2¼	2	1⅞
	3⅜	2¾	2⅜	2¼	2
	3¾	2⅞	2⅝	2⅜	2¼
	4¼	3⅛	2¾	2⅝	2⅜
	4½	3⅜	3	2¾	2⅝
	4¾	3⅝	3¼	2⅞	2¾
	5	3⅞	3⅜	3⅛	2⅞

PROJECTS

1. Dress

Illus. 18.   Front and back views of Pattern 1.

2. Pants

Illus. 19.   Front view of Pattern 2.

Supplies

Yardage based on 45″ width fabric.
¼ yard dress fabric (yardage estimate for Patterns
   1 and 2)
1 spool thread

2 small snaps for lightweight material
3–4 inches ⅛″ width elastic
6 inches ½″ width self-made ruffle or lace
   (optional)

PATTERN 1

Dress for seven-inch doll. Doll dress consists of seven pattern pieces. The skirt panel may be divided into three panels; one piece for the front and two pieces for the back.

Instructions

1. With right sides together, sew shoulder seams of front and back yokes, leaving the center of back open.

2. At this point, sew ruffle or lace to the armhole, if you are using this trim. If trim is omitted, turn under with stitching around the armholes. Set bodice aside.

3. With right sides together, sew front-skirt panels.

4. Gather front-and back-skirt panels.

5. With right sides together, sew front skirt to front yoke. In the same fashion, sew back-skirt panels to back yokes.

6. To close, sew side seams of the dress.

7. To finish, turn under with stitching all the raw edges.

8. Sew snaps on back for closure.

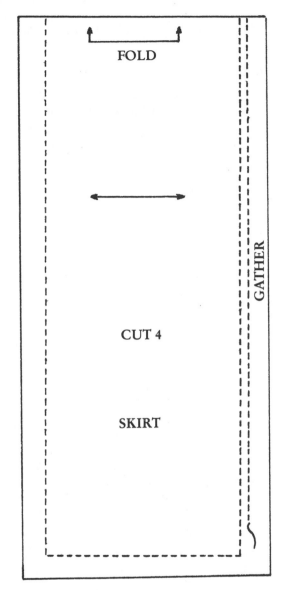

Illus. 20. Pattern 1 for dress.

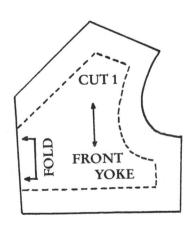

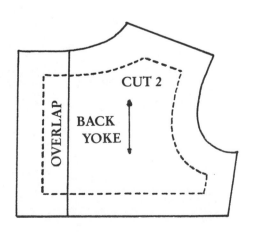

PATTERN 2

Pants for seven-inch doll. This pair of pants consists only of two parts.

Instructions

1. With right sides together, sew crotch of pants.
2. By machine, attach elastic to the waistline of both parts of pants.
3. At this point, finish the hem of pants by turning under with stitching.
4. Sew inner seam of pants.

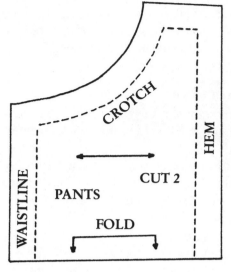

Illus. 21.   Pattern 2 for pants.

3. Gown

Illus. 22.   Front and back views of Pattern 3.

4. Cap

Illus. 23.   Three-quarters view of Pattern 4.

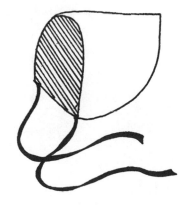

Supplies

Yardage based on 45" width fabric.
¼ yard satin fabric (combined yardage for Patterns 3 and 4)
1 yard ¼" width white lace (optional trim)

1 spool thread
3 small snaps for lightweight material
½ yard ¼" width satin ribbon for cap ties

PATTERN 3

This gown fits an eight-and-a-half inch doll with a toddler-type body. Gown consists of six parts and has a back opening.

Instructions

1. Gather top edge of the front-skirt and back-skirt panels.
2. With right sides together, sew the front skirt to the front yoke.
3. In the same way, sew back-skirt panels to respective back yokes.
4. With right sides together, sew shoulder seams of the front bodice to the back bodice.
5. With right sides together, sew side seams of the gown.
6. To finish, turn under with stitching the raw edges of the back opening and the hem of the dress.
7. Sew lace trim around armholes, neckline, and hem of the gown.
8. For closure, sew snaps on back of gown.

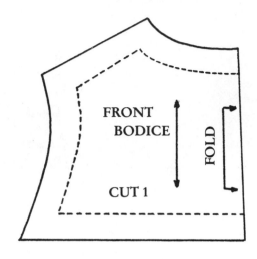

Illus. 24.   Pattern 3 for gown.

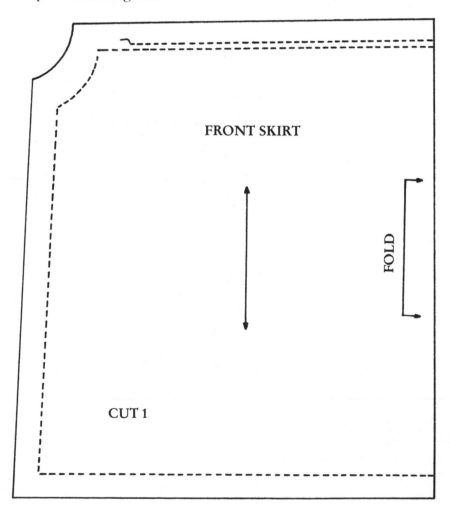

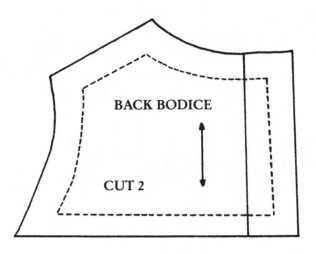

BACK BODICE

CUT 2

Illus. 24 (cont.).

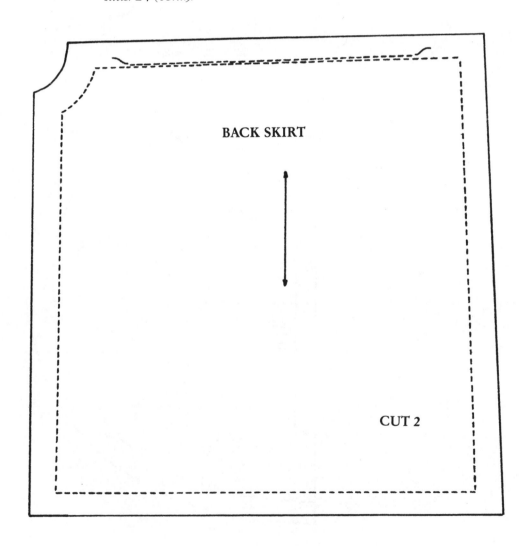

BACK SKIRT

CUT 2

PATTERN 4

This cap fits an eight-and-a-half-inch doll with a head circumference of ten inches. The pattern consists of three parts.

Instructions

1. With right sides together, sew edges of two parts of front together. Turn inside out.
2. Topstitch sewn edges.
3. Sew front to back.
4. To finish the neck edge of the back, turn under with stitching.
5. Attach ribbon ties.

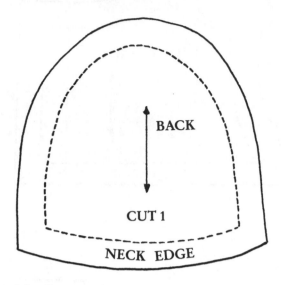

Illus. 25. Pattern 4 for Cap.

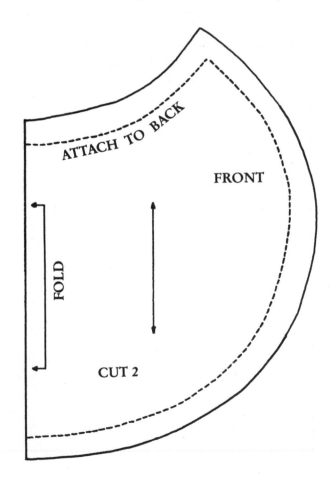

5. Asymmetric Evening Gown
&
6. Pants

Illus. 26. Front and back views of Pattern 5. (Pattern 6 for pants not shown.)

Supplies

Yardage estimates are based on 45″ fabric width.

Pattern 5:

¼ yard satin fabric
1 spool thread
5 small snaps

Pattern 6:

Dress fabric 4½″ × 4½″ square
Sewing thread
¼ yard ⅛″ width elastic

PATTERN 5

This pattern fits a twelve-inch lady-type doll. The evening gown consists primarily of eight pattern pieces. To avoid a seam line on the front skirt, the skirt panel may be divided into three parts: one part for the front panel and two parts for the back panels. Gown has back opening.

Instructions

1. Begin construction by sewing the darts of the bodices; set aside.
2. With right sides together, sew the panels for the front skirt.
3. Gather the skirt panels.
4. Sew the skirt panels to the bodices: front skirt to front bodice and back-skirt panels to back bodices.
5. Gather the sleeve; set aside.
6. With right sides together, sew the front bodice to the back bodice by joining at the one shoulder seam.
7. With right sides together, sew the sleeve to the bodice of gown.
8. At this point, hem the sleeve by turning under with stitching.
9. With right sides together, sew the side seams of the gown.
10. Finish the raw edges by turning under with stitching.
11. For closure, attach snaps on the back of the gown.

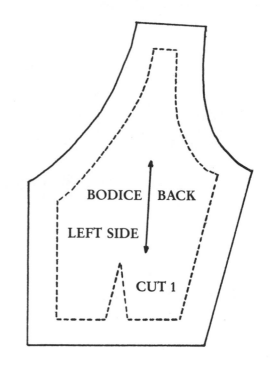

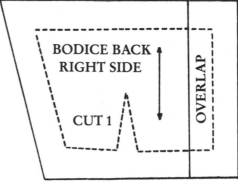

Illus. 27. Pattern 5 for evening gown.

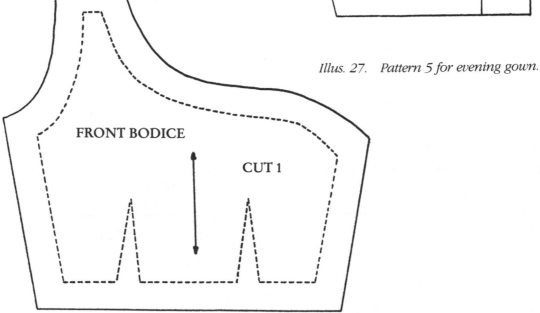

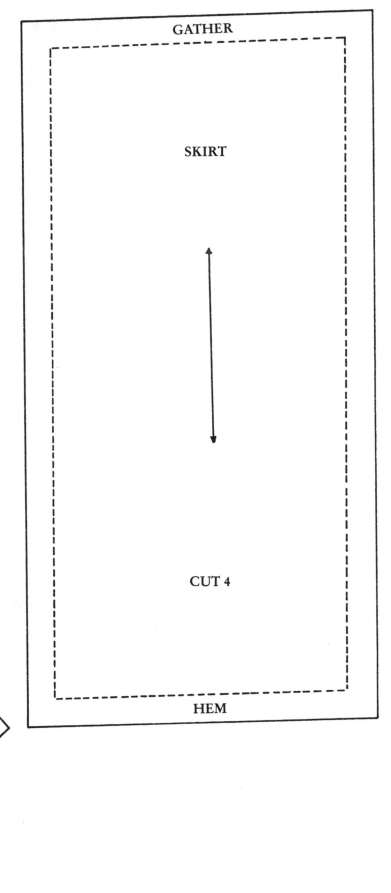

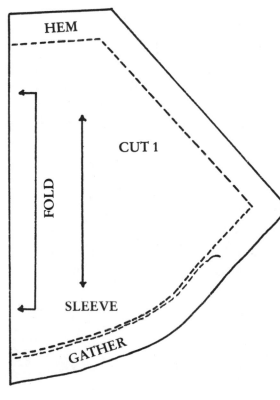

PATTERN 6

This underpants pattern is for an eleven-and-a-half-inch to twelve-inch lady-type doll. Underpants are elasticized at the waist. The pattern consists only of one part.

Instructions

1. Turn under and stitch the hem of the pants.
2. With right sides together, sew the side seams.
3. Attach elastic at the waist.

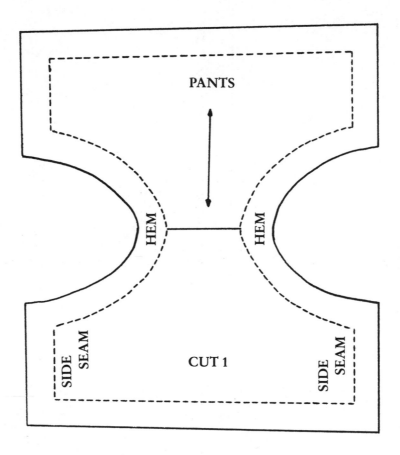

Illus. 28. Pattern 6 for pants.

7. Debut Evening Gown

Illus. 29.   Front and back views of Pattern 7.

Supplies
Yardage estimates are based on 45″ fabric width.
Pattern 7:
¼ yard white veiling
¼ yard satin fabric
1 spool thread
5 small snaps

PATTERN 7

This pattern fits a twelve-inch lady-type doll and consists of nine pattern pieces. To avoid a seam line on the front of the skirt, however, the skirt may be divided into three parts: one part for the front panel and two parts for the back panels. Gown has back opening. Basting is a necessary step if a layered effect is desired; veiling material is satin lined.

Instructions

1. Begin construction by sewing the darts of the bodices.
2. With right sides together, sew the panels for the front skirt. (Eliminate step if a one-piece front panel is desired.)
3. Gather the skirt panels.
4. Sew the skirt panels to the bodices: front skirt to the front bodice and back-skirt panels to back bodices.
5. Gather the sleeves. Set aside.
6. With right sides together, join the shoulder seams of the front bodice to the back-bodice sections.
7. With right sides together, join the sleeves to the bodice of the gown.
8. At this point, hem the sleeves for ease in construction.
9. With right sides together, sew the side seams of the gown.
10. Finish the raw edges by turning under with stitching.
11. For closure, attach snaps on the back of gown.

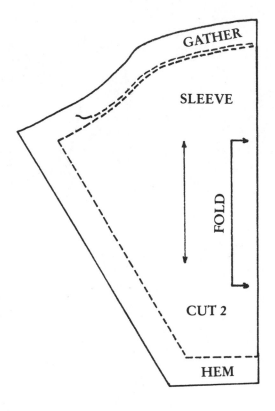

Illus. 30.   Pattern 7 for debut gown.

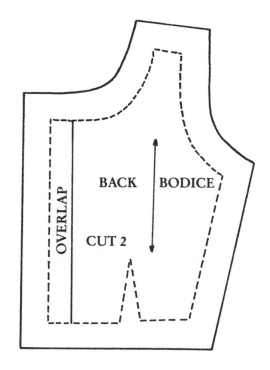

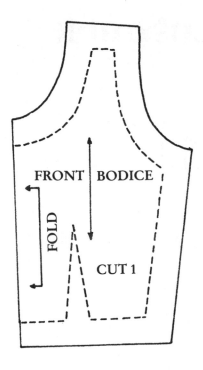

Illus. 30 (cont.).

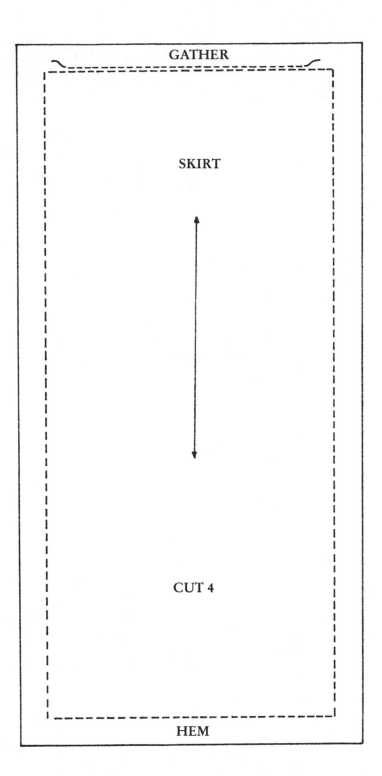

8–10. Gala Gown Ensemble

Illus. 31.   Front and back views of Pattern 8 and Pattern 9.

Illus. 32.   Three-quarters view of Pattern 10.

Supplies
Yardage estimates are based on 45″ fabric width.
Pattern 8, 9, 10:
¼ yard evening dress fabric
6″ × 6″ square veiling
5 small snaps
1 spool thread
Pearl beads and satin ribbon rosettes (optional)

PATTERN 8

This blouse pattern fits a twelve-inch lady-type doll. The blouse is very versatile and can be constructed with different types of materials to suit any setting. The blouse consists of five parts and has a back opening.

Instructions

1. Gather sleeves and set aside.
2. With right sides together, sew the shoulder seams of the front of blouse to the back sections of blouse.
3. With right sides together, sew the sleeves to the blouse.
4. At this point, hem the sleeves for ease in construction.
5. With right sides together, close the side seams of the blouse by sewing from the hem of the blouse to the hem of the sleeves.
6. Finish the raw edges by turning under with stitching.
7. For closure, sew snaps on the back of the blouse.
8. *Optional:* Trim the blouse with pearl beads and satin ribbon rosettes.

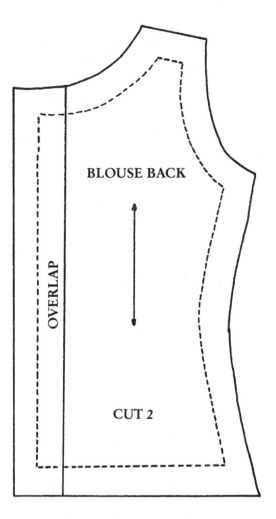

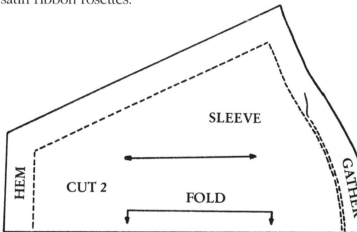

Illus. 33. Pattern 8 for blouse.

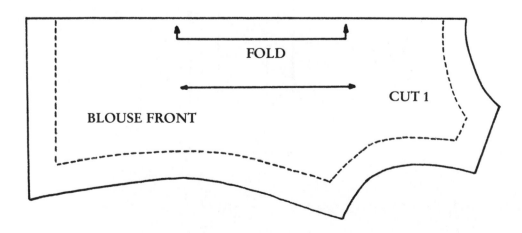

PATTERN 9

This skirt pattern fits a twelve-inch lady-type doll with a waist measurement of three and a half inches. The pattern primarily consists of six parts. To avoid a seam line on the front of the skirt, the skirt may be divided into three parts: one panel for the front and two panels for the back. The skirt can also be cut in one continuous piece. It has a back opening.

Instructions

1. With right sides together, join the panels of the skirt. Remember to leave the back sections unsewn on the center of the back of the skirt for opening.
2. Gather skirt.
3. With right sides together, sew the waistband. Leave one side unsewn for attachment to skirt. Turn inside out.
4. With right sides together, sew the gathered skirt to the waistband.
5. For closure, sew snaps on the back of the skirt.

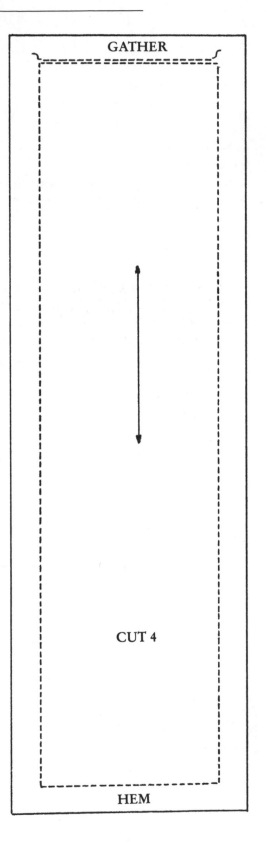

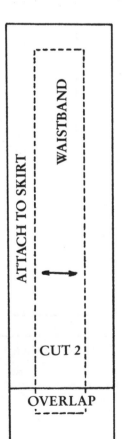

Illus. 34.   Pattern 9 for skirt.

PATTERN 10

This cap fits a twelve-inch lady-type doll with a head circumference of four and a half inches. The cap consists of two pieces.

Instructions

1. Begin construction by sewing the darts of the respective sections.

2. With right sides together, sew the cap leaving one section unsewn to permit turning inside out of the joint parts.
3. Turn inside out.
4. Close the opening with blind stitching.
5. Topstitch the cap.
6. Trim with netting if desired.

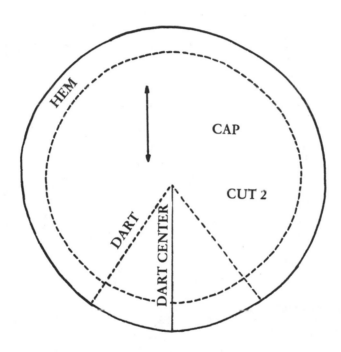

Illus. 35. Pattern 10 for cap.

11–12. Sunsuit/Sundress

Illus. 36.   Front and back views of Pattern 11.

Illus. 37.   Front and back views of Pattern 12.

Supplies

Yardage estimates are based on 45" fabric width.

Pattern 11:

¼ yard dress fabric
3 small snaps
1 spool thread
½ yard ⅛" width ribbon for straps
Optional: 2 inches of ¼" width Venetian lace

Pattern 12:

¼ yard dress fabric
½ yard ⅛" width ribbon for straps
3 small snaps
1 spool thread
Ribbon rosette (optional)

PATTERN 11

This sunsuit fits a twelve-inch lady-type doll. It consists of five parts and has a back opening.

Instructions

1. Begin construction by sewing the darts of the bodices; set aside.
2. With right sides together, sew crotch of the pants. Leave part of the crotch unsewn for part of the back opening.
3. At this point, hem the pants for ease in construction.
4. Sew the inner seams of the pants.
5. Gather the pants; set aside.
6. With right sides together, sew the side seams of the front bodice to the back-bodice sections.
7. With right sides together, join the bodice to the pants.
8. Finish the raw edges by turning under with stitching.
9. Attach ribbon ties for straps.
10. *Optional:* Trim the front of suit with Venetian lace.
11. For closure, sew snaps on the back of the sunsuit.

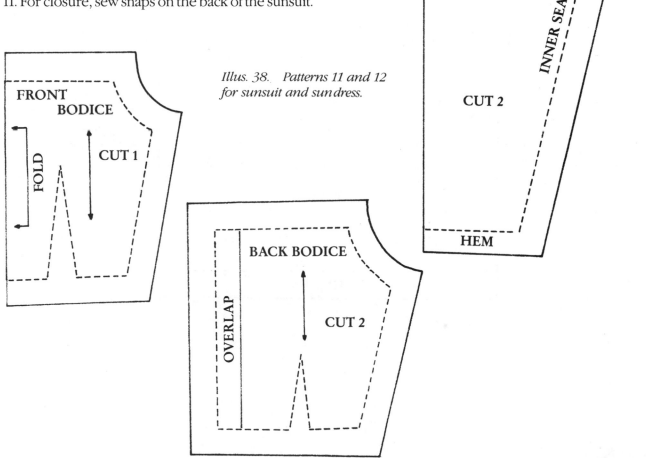

Illus. 38. Patterns 11 and 12 for sunsuit and sundress.

PATTERN 12

This sundress fits a twelve-inch lady-type doll. It consists of seven parts and has a back opening.

Instructions

1. Begin construction by sewing the darts of the bodices; set aside.
2. With right sides together, join the two skirt panels to form the front skirt.
3. Gather the front skirt and the two remaining back-skirt panels.
4. With right sides together, join the skirt panels to the respective bodices.
5. With right sides together, sew the side seams of the front of sundress to the back sections.
6. Finish the raw edges by turning under with stitching.
7. Attach ribbon for straps on shoulders or create your very own self-made shoulder band with the same dress material.
8. *Optional:* Trim the front of the sundress with a ribbon rosette of contrasting color.
9. For closure, sew snaps on back of sundress.

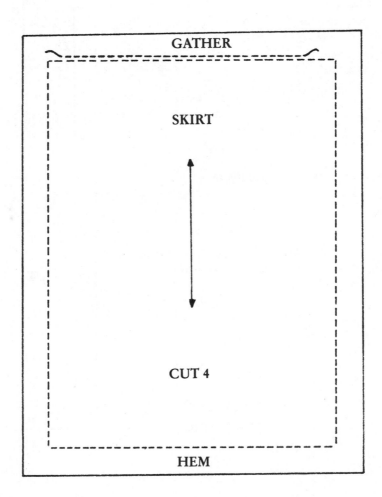

Illus. 38 (cont.).

Fashion-type dolls, from the top clockwise, are wearing gowns made from Patterns 5, 66, 65, 53 and 62.

A

These bridal gowns show a variety of styles. From left to right, the dolls are wearing Patterns 55, 41, 17 and 61.

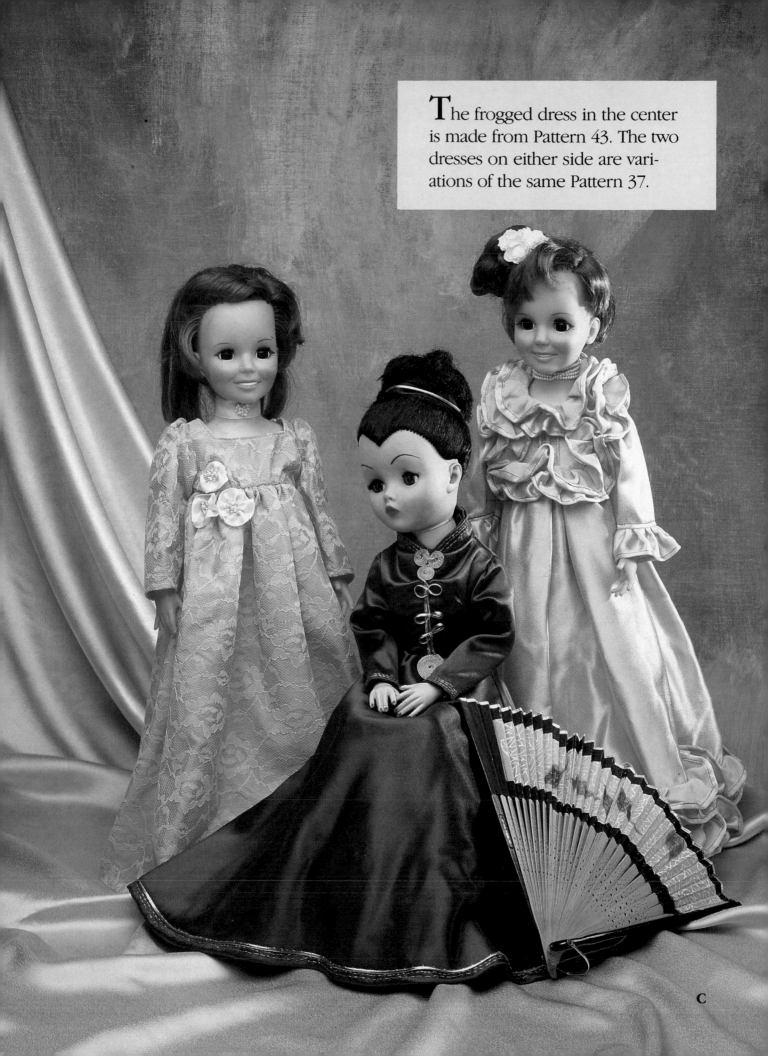

The frogged dress in the center is made from Pattern 43. The two dresses on either side are variations of the same Pattern 37.

C

Dressed for *le sport*, these fashion-type dolls are from left to right, wearing Patterns 63 and 64, 51 and 52, and 59 and 60.

A group of baby and toddler-type dolls, from left to right, are wearing Patterns 23 and 24, 2, and 71 and 72. The toddler-type doll is the smallest.

E

From left to right,
on facing page,
these two popular
dolls are wearing
Patterns 73 and 69.

The two examples
below are wearing
(left) Patterns 27 and 28
and (right) Patterns 67
and 68.

These three show
some of the wide vari-
ety of doll sizes and
shapes, as well as the
extensive wardrobe.
From left to right, they
are wearing Patterns
29, 3 and 4, and 33, 34,
35 and 36.

H

13. Doll Body

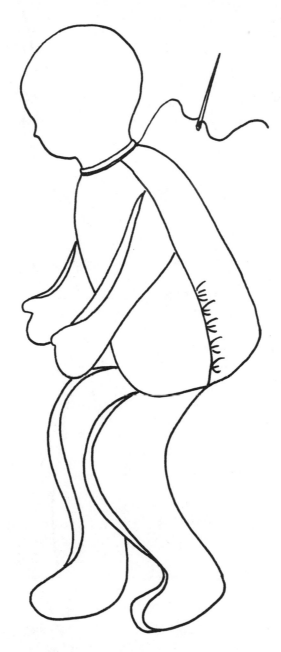

Illus. 39.   Side view of Pattern 13.

Supplies

Yardage based on 45″ width fabric.
¼ yard unbleached muslin (calico)
1 spool thread
14 inches ¹⁄₁₆″-gauge wire or nylon cord (neck and arms only)
Loose polyester or cotton batting

PATTERN 13

This bodice pattern is for a twelve-inch doll with or without the lower parts of arms and legs. Total number of parts for this pattern is six pieces.

Instructions

1. With right sides together, sew two sets of arms. Sew around the perimeter, leaving top edge open (towards body). Cut excess fabric and turn inside out.

2. With right sides together, sew two sets of legs. Sew around the perimeter, leaving top edge open (towards body). Cut excess fabric and turn inside out.

3. Stuff with cotton or polyester batting (legs and arms), leaving about one-quarter inch room for attachment.

4. Baste down the opening of parts for ease in attachment to the body; set aside parts.

5. Gather bodice back until the body length matches with the front piece. The extra length of the fabric, when gathered, allows the doll to sit.

7. Sew darts together on both front and back bodices.

8. With right sides together, sew front and back of bodice together. Turn inside out.

9. Fold a portion of the neck area and sew one-quarter inch from the edge. This will allow a string or thin wire to pass through for head attachment.

10. Attach arms and legs to the bodice.

11. Stuff the body.

12. Run the wire or cord through the neck area. Twist wire or tie the cord securely to the head flange of the doll.

Note: For dolls with hands and feet, cut unwanted areas and repeat steps 9 and 12.

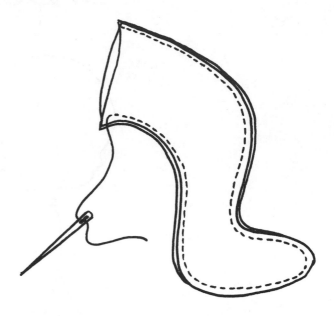

Illus. 41. Sewing the legs of the doll body.

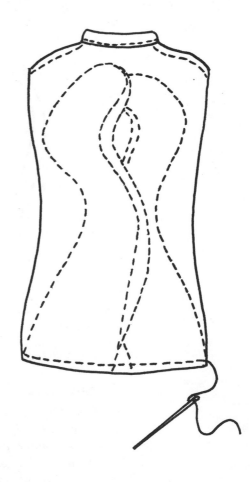

Illus. 42. Attaching the legs to the body. With right sides together, stuffed legs in position, sew the front body to the back body as illustrated.

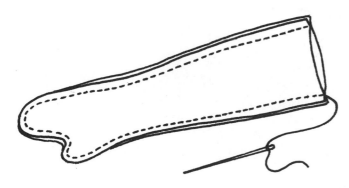

Illus. 40. Sewing the arms of the doll body.

34   **Doll Body**

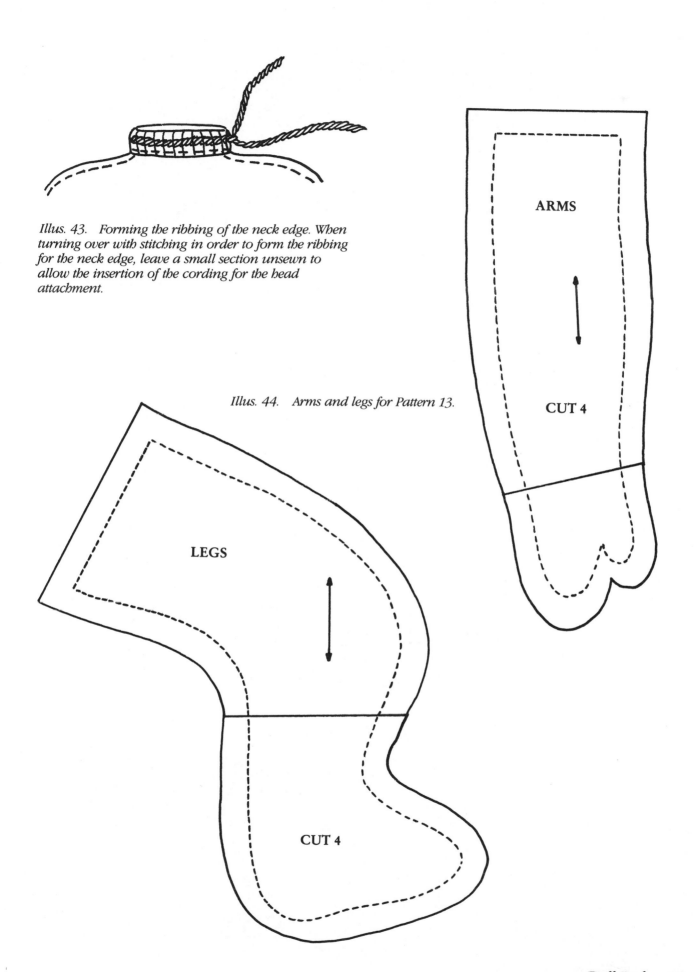

Illus. 43.   Forming the ribbing of the neck edge. When turning over with stitching in order to form the ribbing for the neck edge, leave a small section unsewn to allow the insertion of the cording for the head attachment.

Illus. 44.   Arms and legs for Pattern 13.

ARMS

CUT 4

LEGS

CUT 4

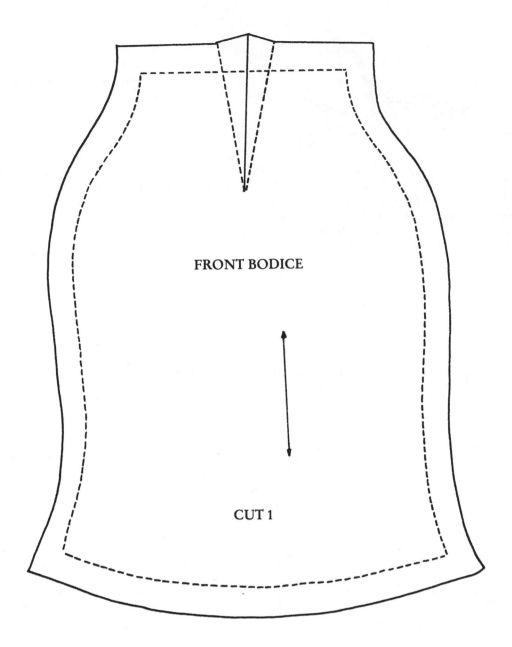

Illus. 45. Front bodice for Pattern 13.

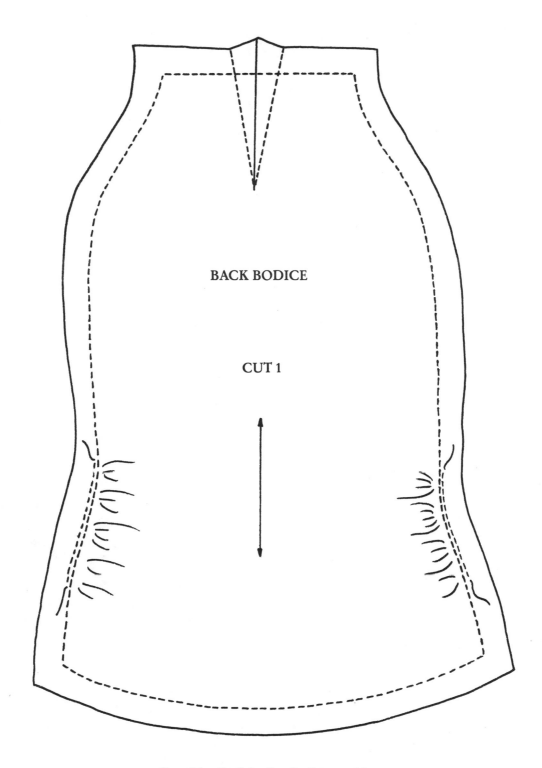

BACK BODICE

CUT 1

Illus. 46. Back bodice for Pattern 13.

14. Dress

Illus. 47.   Front and back views of Pattern 14.

15. Pants

16. Bonnet

Illus. 49.   Front, side and back views of Pattern 16.

Illus. 48.   Front view of Pattern 15.

Supplies
Yardage based on 45" width fabric.
*1 yard dress fabric (combined yardage estimate
    for Patterns 14, 15 and 16)*
1 spool thread
⅓ yard ⅛" width elastic
1⅔ yards ¼" width lace for trimming (optional)
3 small snaps for lightweight material

PATTERN 14

This pattern is for a twelve-inch baby-type doll. The garment consists of nine pattern pieces. The skirt panel may be divided into three parts; one part for the front panel and two for the back panels. This dress may be constructed with or without sleeves and has a back opening.

Instructions

1. With right sides together, sew two panels of pieces to form the front panel of the skirt. If cutting one piece for the front skirt, omit this step.
2. Gather the front skirt and back panels. Remember to leave the center back of the back-skirt panels unsewn.
3. With right sides together, sew the front panel of the skirt to the front yoke. In the same way, sew the back-skirt panels to the back yokes.
4. With right sides together, sew shoulder seams of the front of the dress to the back of the dress.
5. With right sides together, sew the side seams of the dress.
6. *Optional:* Finish the edges with lace trimming.
7. For closure, attach snaps on the back of the dress.

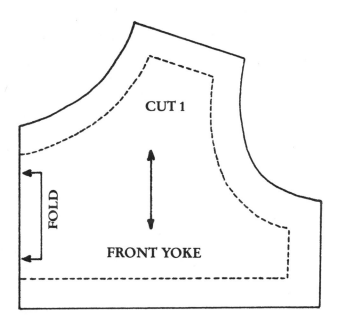

Illus. 50.   Pattern 14 for dress.

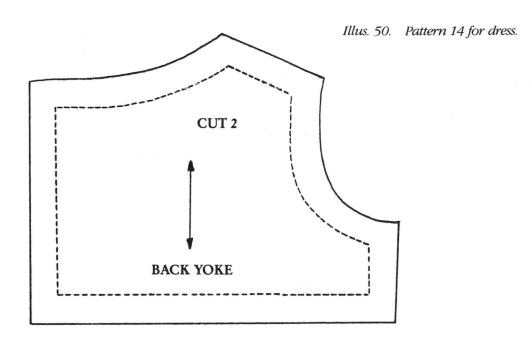

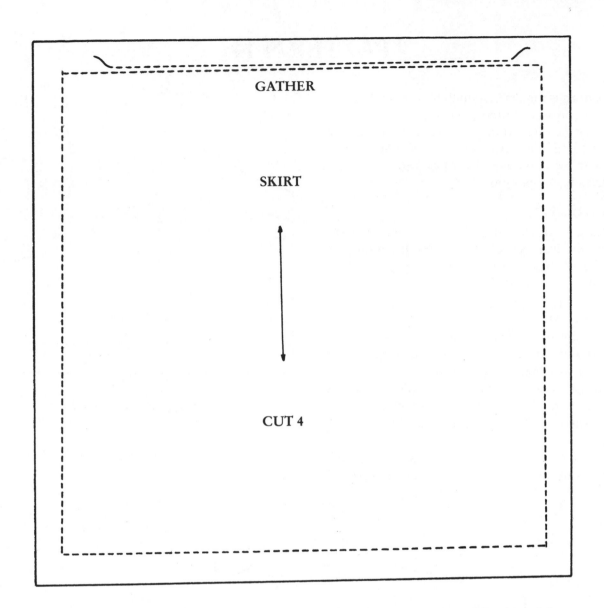

GATHER

SKIRT

CUT 4

Illus. 51.   Pattern 14 for skirt of dress.

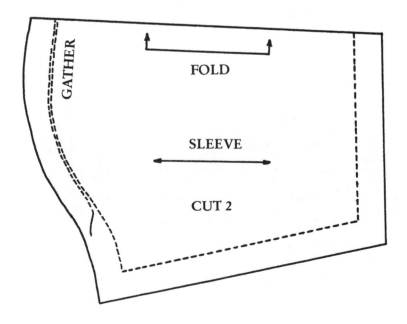

GATHER

FOLD

SLEEVE

CUT 2

PATTERN 15

This pattern is for the undergarment of a twelve-inch baby doll. There are four pattern pieces.

Instructions

1. With right sides together, sew crotch areas to form front and back of pants.
2. With right sides together, sew side seams of underpants.
3. With right sides together, sew inner seam of pants.
4. Sew elastic on waistline by machine. (If sewing by hand, fold and sew about one-quarter inch on waist and leg areas, allowing enough room to allow for elastic insertion.) In the same way, sew elastic on the leg circumference of pants.

Note: This pattern is designed for a "sit-down" doll.

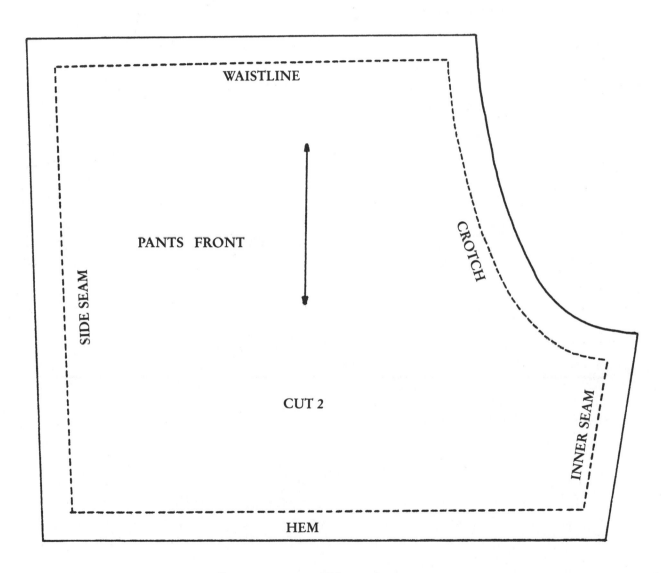

Illus. 52. Pattern 15 for undergarment.

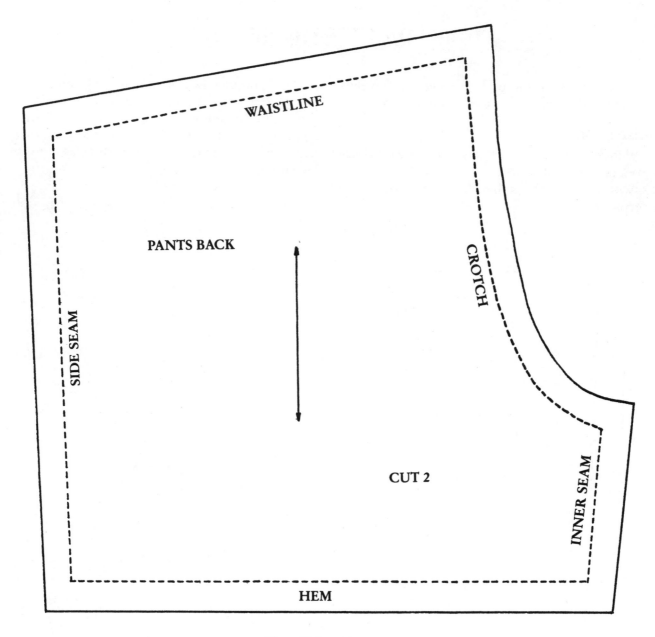

WAISTLINE

PANTS BACK

SIDE SEAM

CROTCH

CUT 2

INNER SEAM

HEM

Illus. 52 (cont.).

PATTERN 16

This baby bonnet fits a twelve-inch baby-type doll with a head circumference of twelve inches. Bonnet consists of two pattern pieces.

Instructions

1. With right sides together, sew the center-back seam of bonnet.
2. With right sides together, sew top seam of bonnet.
3. Trim bonnet with lace around the bonnet's front edge.
4. Sew ribbon ties.

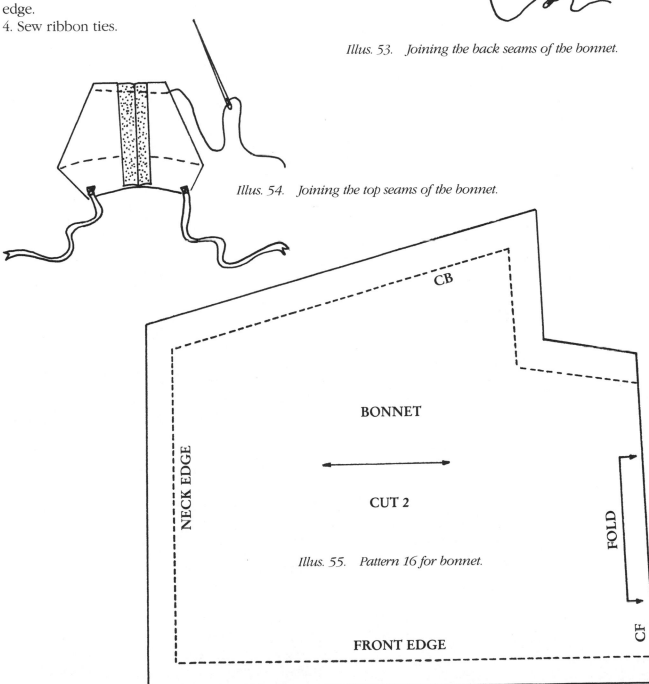

Illus. 53.   Joining the back seams of the bonnet.

Illus. 54.   Joining the top seams of the bonnet.

Illus. 55.   Pattern 16 for bonnet.

17. Bridal Gown

Illus. 56.   Front and back views of Pattern 17.

18. Veil

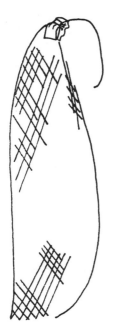

Illus. 57.   Side view of Pattern 18.

19. Pants

Illus. 58.   Front view of Pattern 19.

Supplies
¼ yard net veiling
½ yard lace fabric
¼ yard lining fabric
1 spool white thread
8 inches ¼" width elastic beads (optional)
3 small snaps for medium-weight material
1 packaged single-fold white bias tape

PATTERN 17

This bridal gown fits a twelve-inch doll with a girl-type body. The gown consists of eleven parts. The skirt panels may be cut in a full circle as diagrammed in the pattern. Gown has back opening.

Instructions

1. With right sides together, sew the side seams of the first layer of the front skirt to the first layer of the back skirt.

2. With right sides together, finish the first layer of the skirt by turning under with stitching or by trimming with bias tape.

3. Repeat instructions 1 and 2 for construction of the second layer of the skirt; set aside.

4. With right sides together, sew the shoulder seams of the front bodice to the back bodice; set aside.

5. Gather sleeves.

6. With right sides together, sew sleeves into the bodice.

7. At this point, finish the sleeves at the wrist by turning under with stitching or by trimming bias binding.

8. Close side seams of the bodice from the hem of sleeves to the waistline.

9. With right sides together, join the bodice to the skirt of the dress.

10. Finish raw edges (neck and center-back seams) with bias binding.

11. Attach snaps on back for closure.

12. *Optional:* Sew beads on dress.

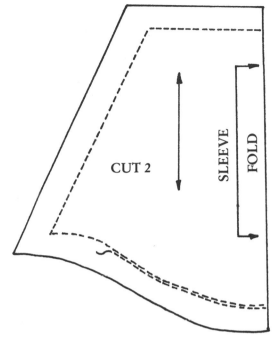

Illus. 59.   Pattern 17 for bridal gown.

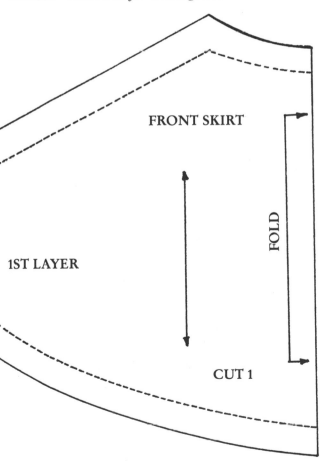

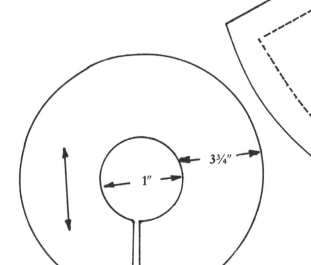

FULL-CIRCLE DIAGRAM

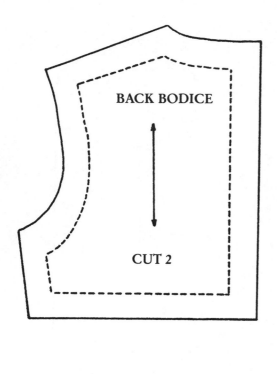

BACK BODICE

CUT 2

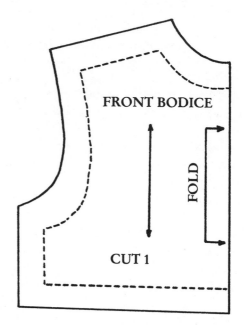

FRONT BODICE

FOLD

CUT 1

Illus. 59 (cont.).

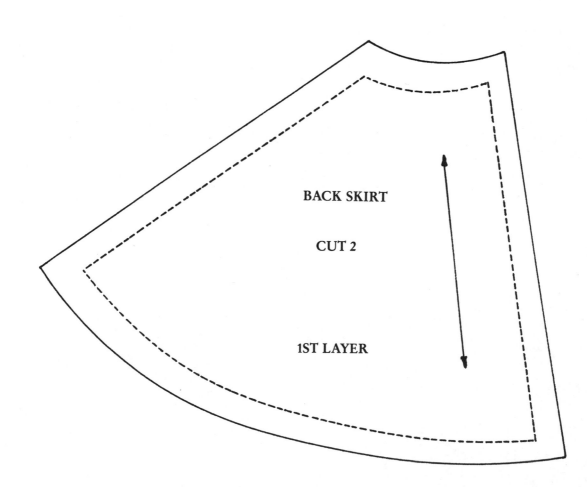

BACK SKIRT

CUT 2

1ST LAYER

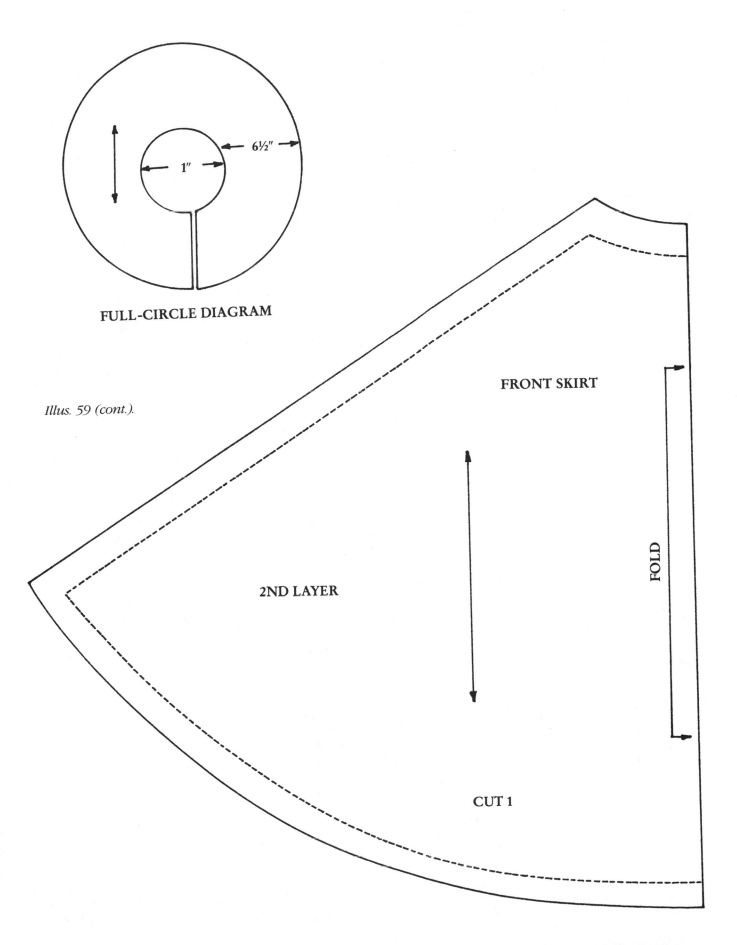

FULL-CIRCLE DIAGRAM

1"

6½"

Illus. 59 (cont.).

FRONT SKIRT

2ND LAYER

FOLD

CUT 1

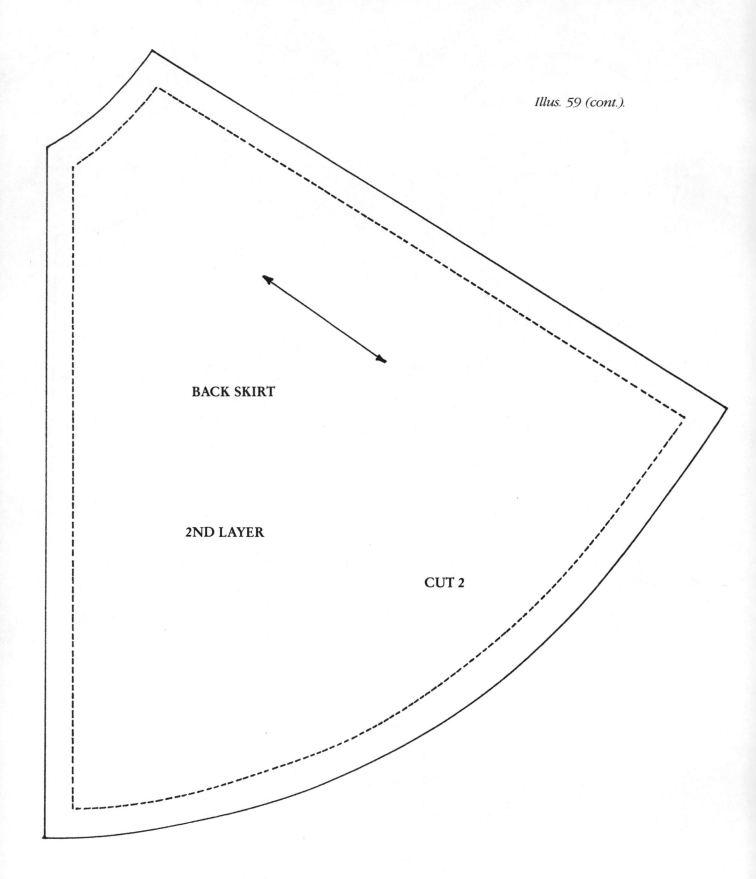

BACK SKIRT

2ND LAYER

CUT 2

PATTERN 18

This veiling fits a twelve-inch doll with a girl-type body.

Instructions

1. Gather veiling at the shortest point, about one inch from the edge.

2. Trim the veiling at the gathered section with a satin bow.

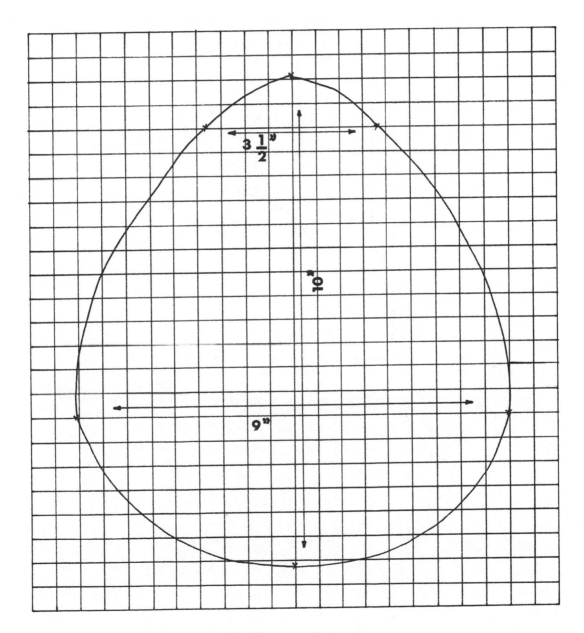

ONE SQUARE = ½ INCH

Illus. 60.   Pattern for wedding veil.

PATTERN 19

These pants fit a twelve-inch doll with a girl-type body. The pants consist only of two pieces.

Instructions

1. With right sides together, sew side seams.
2. At this point, finish the hem of the pants by turning under with stitching or by trimming with lace.
3. With right sides together, sew inner seams of pants.
4. By machine or by hand, attach elastic to waistline.

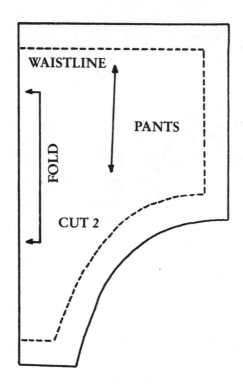

Illus. 61.   Pattern 19 for pants.

20. Bonnet

Illus. 64.   Side view of Pattern 20.

21. Pinafore

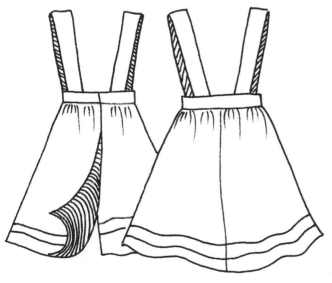

Illus. 63.   Front and back views of Pattern 21.

22. Dress

Illus. 62.   Front and back views of Pattern 22.

Supplies

Yardage based on 45" width fabric.

*½ yard dress fabric (combined yardage estimate
   for Patterns 20 and 22 only)*
¼ yard fabric for pinafore
1 spool thread

3 small snaps for lightweight material
*1 yard ⅛" width double-faced satin ribbon for
   pinafore trim (optional)*
3½ yards ¼" width lace for trimming (optional)

PATTERN 20

This bonnet fits a thirteen-inch doll with a head circumference of thirteen inches. Bonnet has four parts.

Instructions

1. With right sides together, sew the two parts of brim together. Turn inside out.
2. Topstitch brim.
3. Sew back seam of bonnet.
4. Sew bonnet to brim.
5. Sew ribbon ties to the base of the bonnet.
6. *Optional:* Trim bonnet with lace.

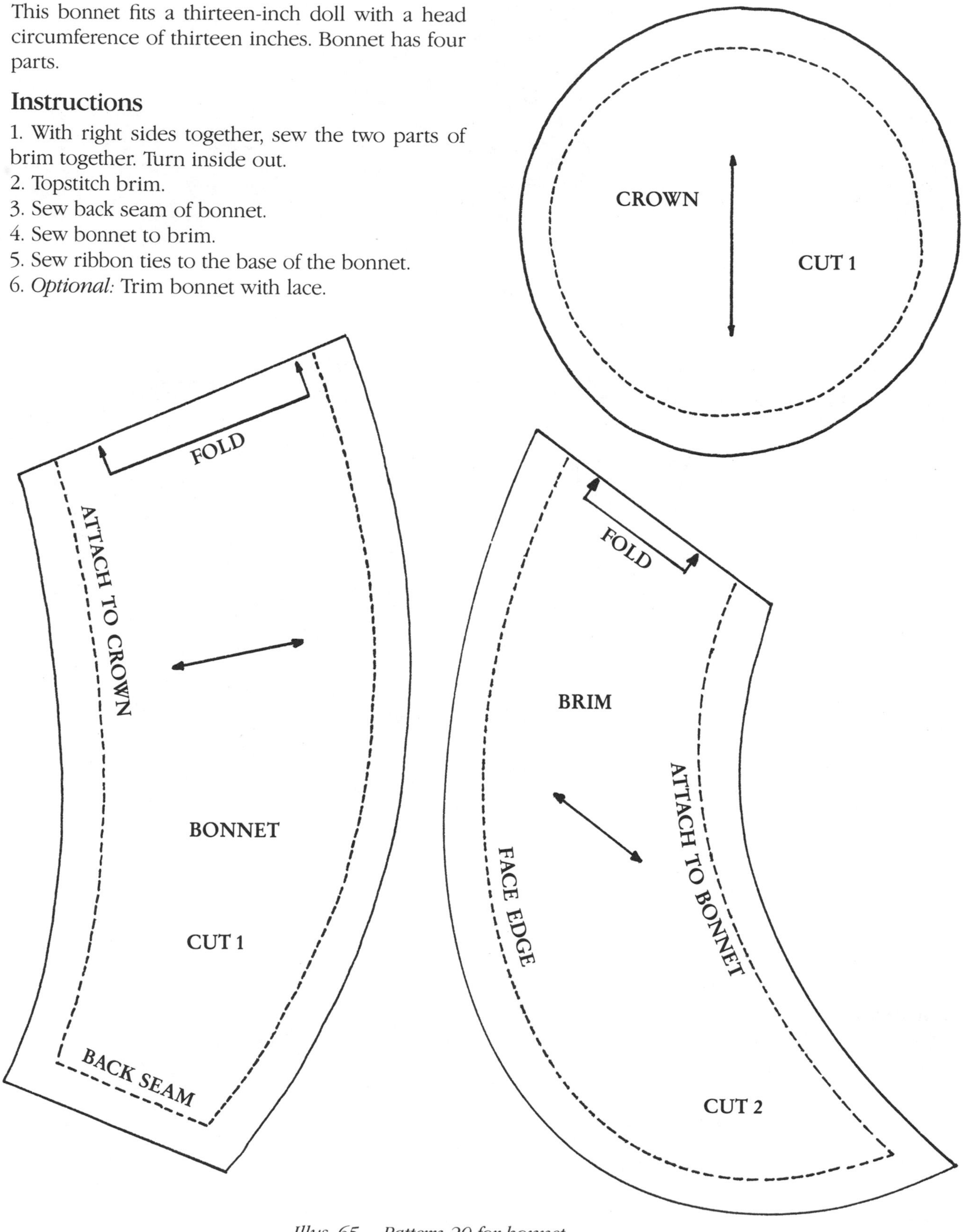

CROWN

CUT 1

FOLD

ATTACH TO CROWN

BONNET

CUT 1

BACK SEAM

FOLD

BRIM

ATTACH TO BONNET

FACE EDGE

CUT 2

Illus. 65. Pattern 20 for bonnet.

PATTERN 21

This pinafore fits a thirteen-inch doll with a girl-type body. Pinafore consists of eleven parts and has a back opening.

Instructions

1. With right sides together, sew end seams of waistband and turn inside out. Set aside.
2. With right sides together, sew skirt panels together, leaving back seam open.
3. Gather skirt of pinafore.
4. With right sides together, sew waistband to the skirt.
5. With right sides together, sew three sides of the front bib. Turn inside out. The open end will be sewn to the waistband.
6. Sew front-bodice panel to the waistband. (Match center of waistband to the center of the front-bodice panel.)
7. Sew shoulder bands together (two sets). Sew all three sides, leaving one end open for turning inside out. Turn inside out.
8. With right sides together, sew shoulder bands to pinafore, placing one end of the band on the front bodice and the other band on the back of pinafore.
9. Sew hooks and eyes on back for closure.
10. *Optional:* Trim pinafore with ribbon.

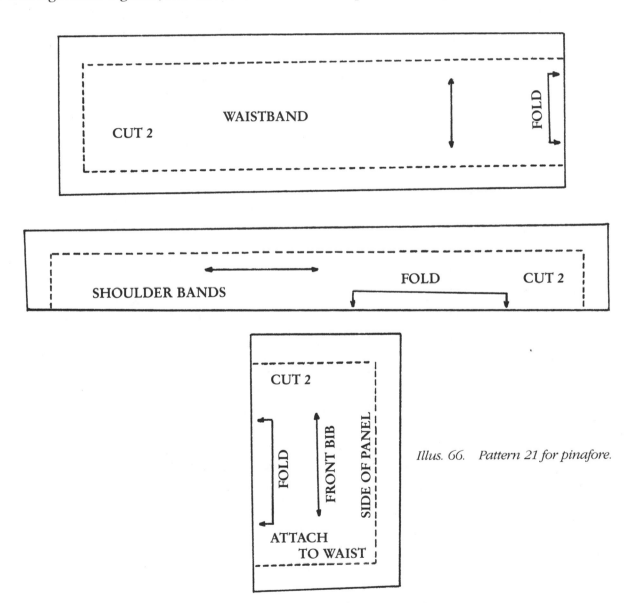

Illus. 66.   Pattern 21 for pinafore.

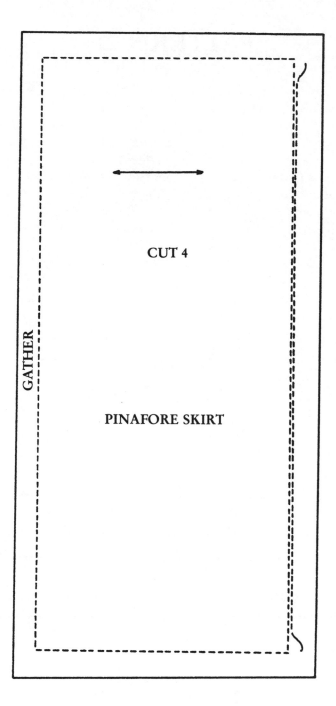

Illus. 66 (cont.).

PATTERN 22

This dress fits a thirteen-inch doll with a girl-type body. Dress consists of ten parts and has a back opening.

Instructions

1. With right sides together, sew two panels of skirt to form one front panel.
2. Gather skirt panels and sleeves.
3. With right sides together, sew front-skirt panel to the front bodice. In the same fashion, sew back-skirt panels to back bodices.
4. With right sides together, sew sleeves into the bodice.
5. *Optional:* Attach elastic to sleeve hem at this point.
6. Turn under with stitching the outer edges of the collar.
7. With right sides together, sew collar to dress.
8. With right sides together, sew side seams of dress.
9. To finish, turn under with stitching all the raw edges of the dress.
10. *Optional:* Trim skirt and collar with gathered lace.

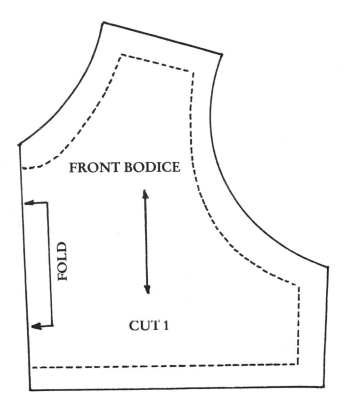

Illus. 67.   Pattern 22 for dress.

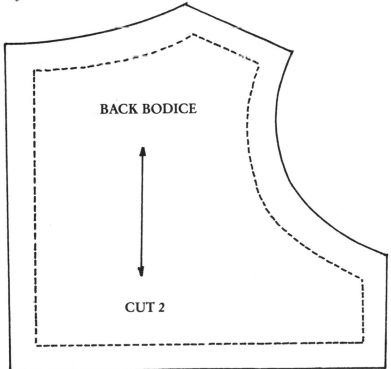

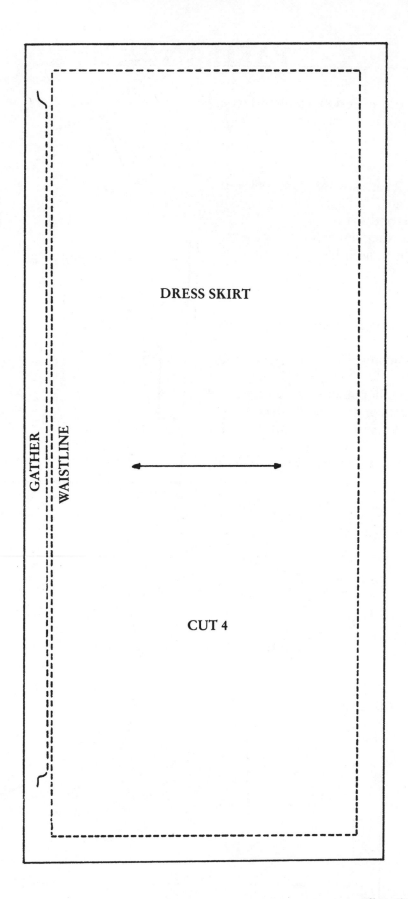

DRESS SKIRT

GATHER

WAISTLINE

CUT 4

Illus. 67 (cont.).

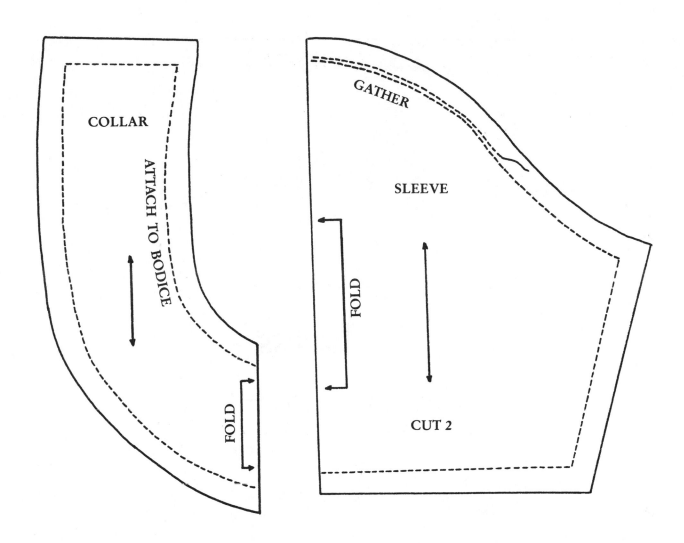

COLLAR

ATTACH TO BODICE

FOLD

GATHER

SLEEVE

FOLD

CUT 2

Illus. 67 (cont.).

23. Bonnet

Illus. 68. Front and back views of Pattern 24.

24. Dress

Illus. 69. Front and back views of Pattern 23.

Supplies

Yardage based on 45″ width fabric.

*½ yard fabric (combined yardage estimate for
    Patterns 23 and 24)*

1 spool thread

6 inches ⅛″ width elastic

2 yards ½″ width lace (optional)

½ yard ¼″ width double-faced satin ribbon

3 small snaps for lightweight material

PATTERN 23

This baby bonnet fits a fifteen-inch baby-type doll with a head circumference of thirteen inches. The bonnet consists of two pieces.

Instructions

1. With right sides together, sew bonnet front to bonnet back.
2. Turn under with stitching, the front edge of the bonnet front and neck edge.
3. Sew ribbon ties.
4. *Optional:* Trim bonnet with lace.

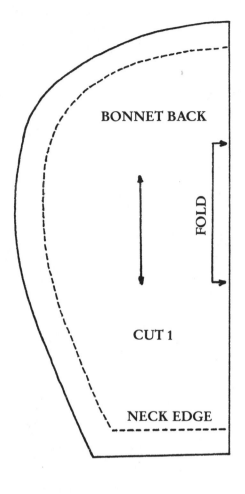

BONNET BACK

FOLD

CUT 1

NECK EDGE

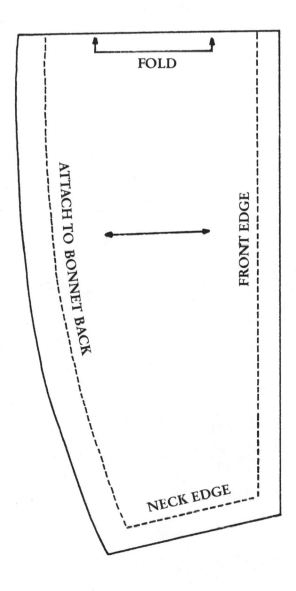

FOLD

ATTACH TO BONNET BACK

FRONT EDGE

NECK EDGE

Illus. 70.   Pattern 23 for bonnet.

PATTERN 24

This doll-baby dress pattern fits a twelve-inch or fifteen-inch doll. Dress length and sleeves may be extended. Dress consists of eight pieces and has a back opening.

Instructions

1. Gather front skirt, back-skirt panels and sleeves; set aside.
2. With right sides together, sew front yoke to gathered front skirt.
3. With right sides together, sew back yokes to back-skirt panels.
4. With right sides together, sew shoulder seams of front yoke to back yokes.

5. With right sides together, sew sleeves to bodice.
6. At this point, trim the sleeves with lace (if applicable).
7. Sew elastic on the wrist of sleeves by machine.
8. With right sides together, sew side seams of front bodice to the back bodice.
9. Finish back panels, hem, neckline and center-back opening by turning under with stitching.
10. *Optional:* Finish remaining edges with lace trimming.
11. Sew snaps on back for closure.

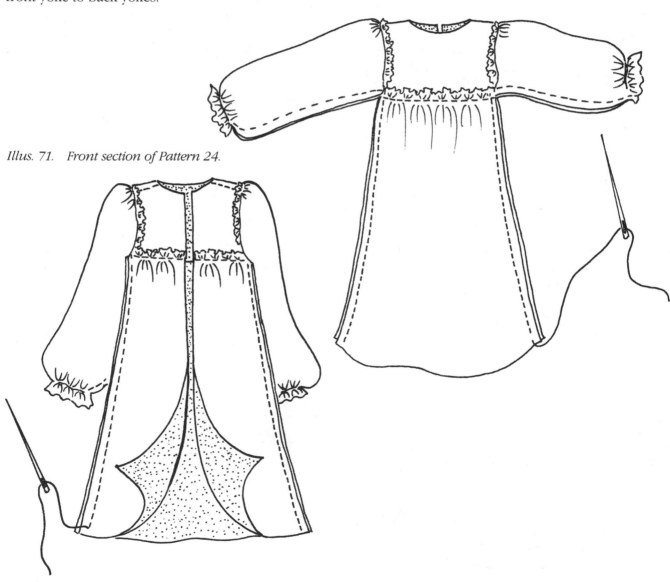

Illus. 71. Front section of Pattern 24.

Illus. 72. Back section of Pattern 24.

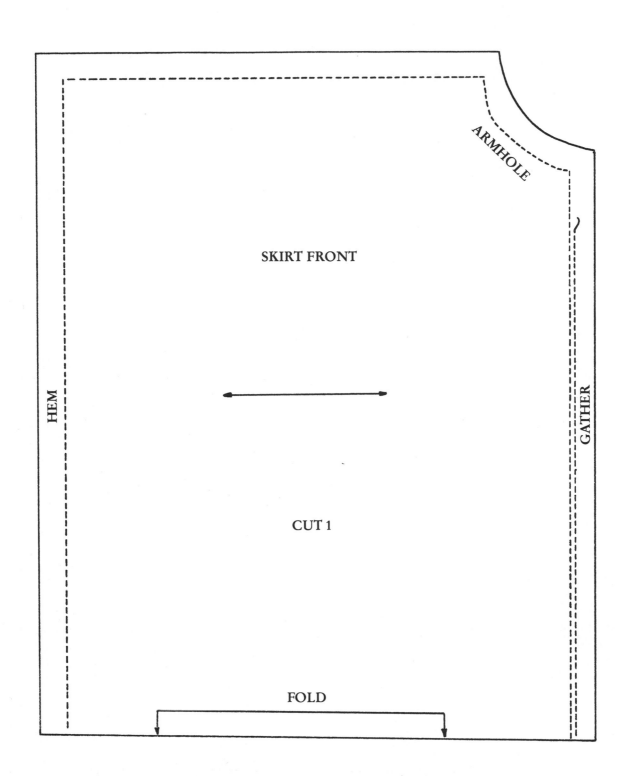

Illus. 73.   Pattern 24 for dress.

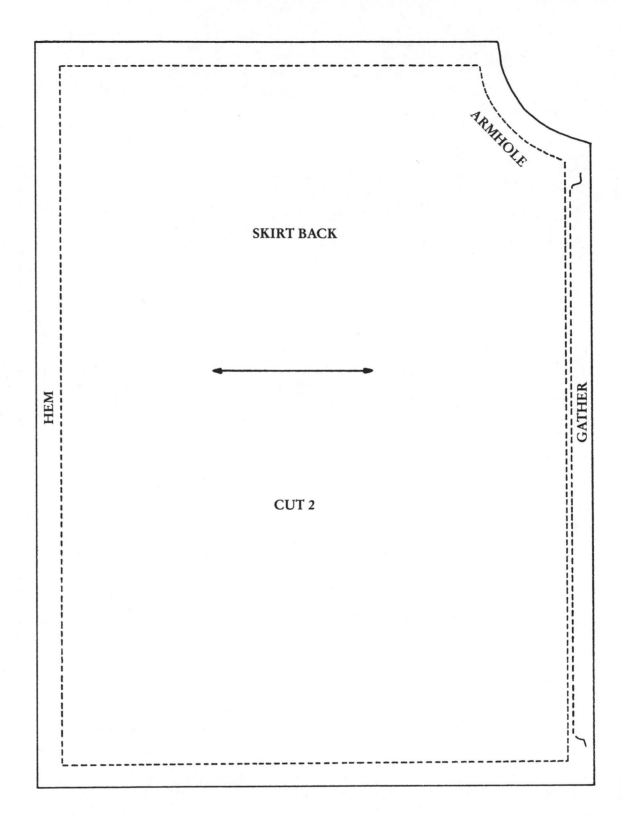

SKIRT BACK

CUT 2

ARMHOLE

GATHER

HEM

Illus. 73 (cont.).

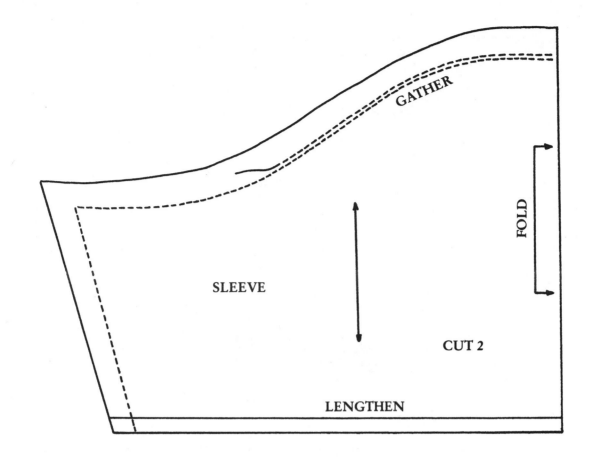

SLEEVE

GATHER

FOLD

CUT 2

LENGTHEN

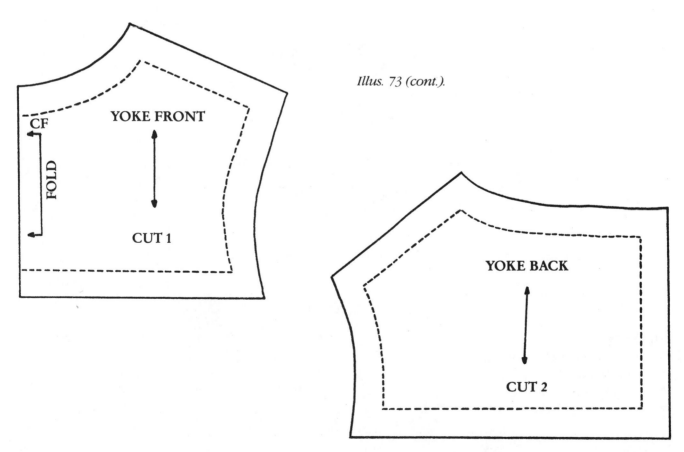

YOKE FRONT

CF

FOLD

CUT 1

Illus. 73 (cont.).

YOKE BACK

CUT 2

Dress 63

25. Dress

Illus. 74.   Front and back views of Pattern 25.

26. Pants

Illus. 75.   Front view of Pattern 26.

Supplies
yardage based on 45″ width fabric.
*¼ yard lavender velvet fabric (combined yardage
    for Patterns 25 and 26)*
½ yard ½″ width satin ribbon for dress sash

*½ yard ¼″ width scalloped lace for the neck and
    armhole edging.*
1 spool lavender thread
3 small snaps for medium-weight material
12 inches ¼″ width elastic for pants

This dress fits a fifteen-inch doll with a teen-type body. It consists of three parts: one piece for the front and two pieces for the back. Dress has back opening.

Instructions

1. With right sides together, sew shoulder seams of front bodice to the back bodice.

2. At this point, trim the neck edge and armholes with the scalloped lace.
3. With right sides together, sew the side seams of the dress.
4. Finish back opening and hem of dress by turning under with stitching.
5. Attach sashing to the dress.
6. For closure, sew snaps on back of the dress.

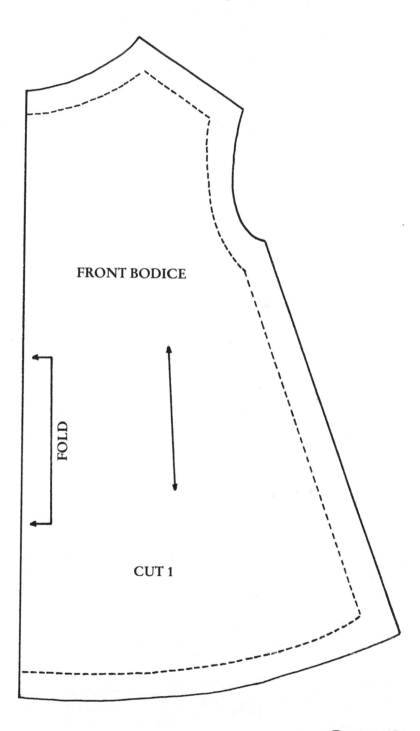

FRONT BODICE

FOLD

CUT 1

Illus. 76.   Pattern 25 for dress.

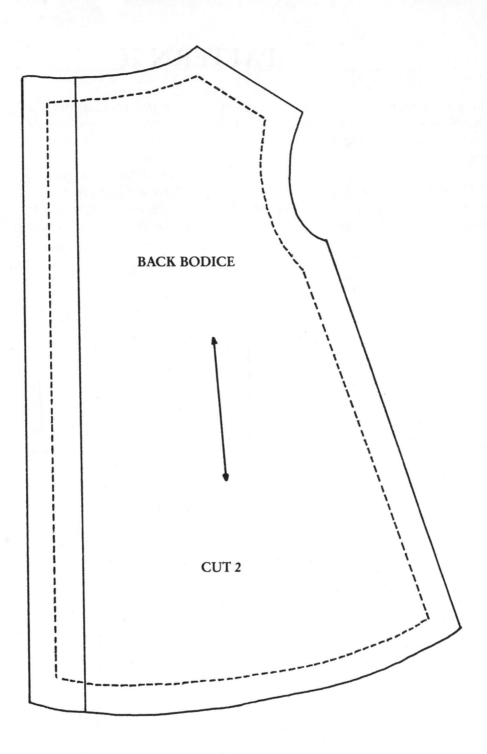

BACK BODICE

CUT 2

Illus. 76 (cont.).

PATTERN 26

These pants fit a fifteen-inch doll with a teen-type body. Pants consist only of two parts.

Instructions

1. Hem the pants by turning under with stitching. Attach lace if desired.
2. With right sides together, sew the side seams of the pants.
3. With right sides together, sew the inner seams of pants.
4. Attach elastic to waistline.

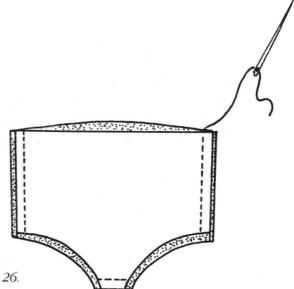

Illus. 77.   Construction diagram for Pattern 26.

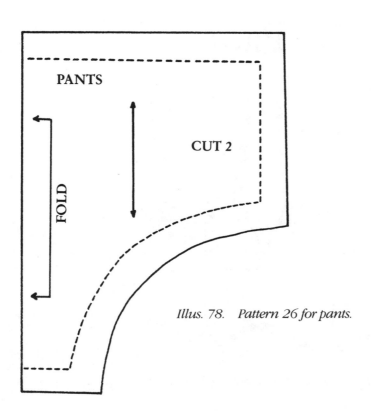

PANTS

FOLD

CUT 2

Illus. 78.   Pattern 26 for pants.

27. Shirt

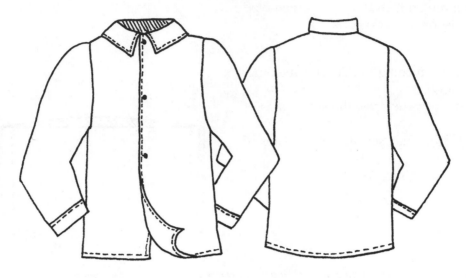

Illus. 79.   Front and back views of Pattern 27.

28. Pants

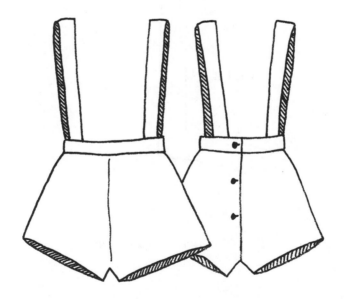

Illus. 80.   Front and back views of Pattern 28.

Supplies

Yardage estimate based on 45″ width fabric.

Pattern 27

¼ yard shirting fabric
2 inches Velcro fastening tape
1 spool thread

Pattern 28

¼ yard medium-weight fabric
2 small snaps
1 spool thread

PATTERN 27

This shirt fits a fifteen-inch baby-type cloth-body doll. The shirt consists of seven parts and has a front opening.

Instruction

1. With right sides together, form the collar, leaving the neckline seam unsewn. Set aside.
2. With right sides together, sew the shoulder seams of the front sections of the shirt to the back section. Set aside.
3. Gather the sleeves.
4. At this point, hem the sleeves for ease of construction. Set aside.
5. With right sides together, sew the collar to the shirt.
6. With right sides together, sew the sleeves to the shirt.
7. With right sides together, sew the side seams of the shirt starting from the hem of the sleeves to the hem of the shirt.
8. Finish the raw edges by turning under with stitching.
9. For closure, sew Velcro on the front of the shirt.

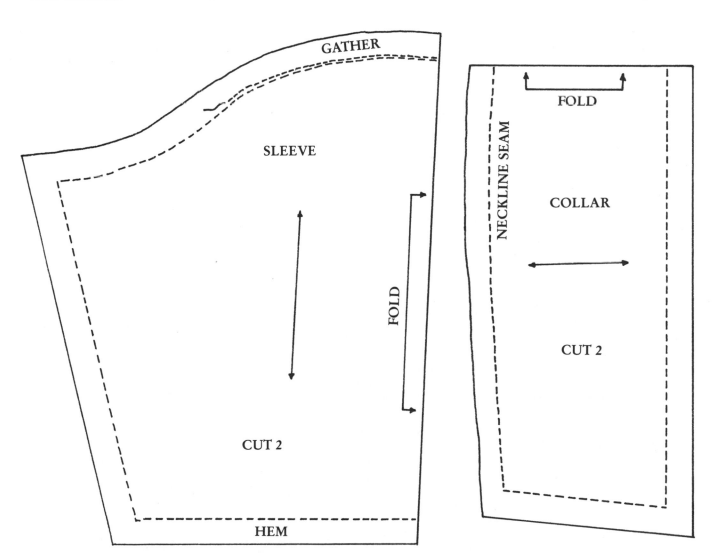

Illus. 81. Pattern 27 for shirt.

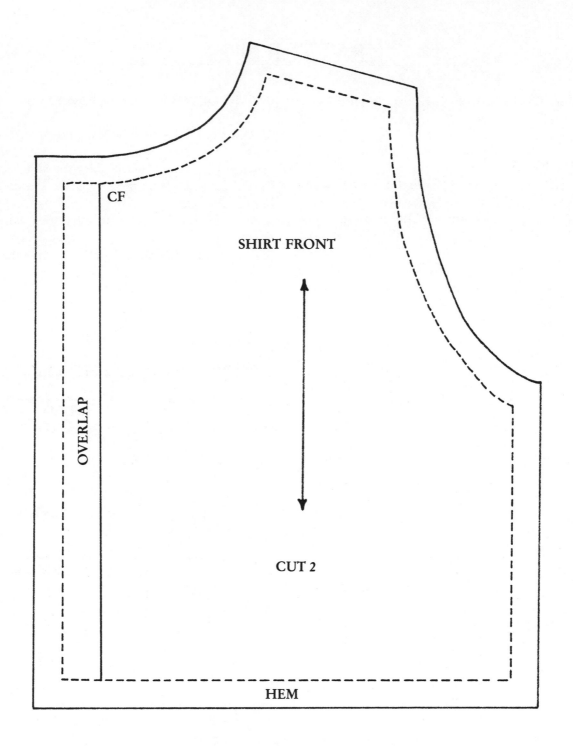

Illus. 81 (cont.).

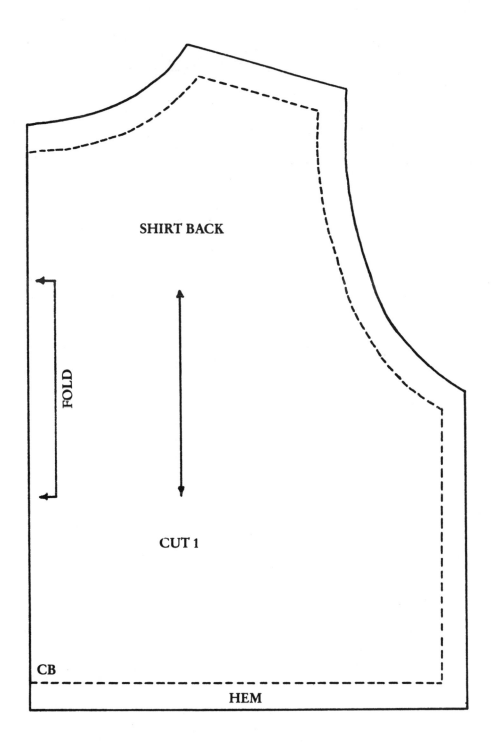

SHIRT BACK

FOLD

CUT 1

CB

HEM

Illus. 81 (cont.).

PATTERN 28

This pants pattern fits a fifteen-inch baby-type doll with a cloth body. The pants consist of eight parts and have a back opening. For a girl-type doll of this classification, attach elastic to the waistline and hem of pants to form pantaloon underpants.

Instructions

1. With right sides together, sew the crotch of the pants. Leave one section of the crotch unsewn for part of the back opening (see Illus. 16).
2. At this point, hem the pants by turning under with stitching.
3. With right sides together, sew the inner seams of the pants; set aside.
4. With right sides together, form the waistband, leaving one long seam unsewn. Turn inside out.
5. With right sides together, sew the waistband to the pants.
6. With right sides together, form the two sets of suspenders. Turn inside out. Suspenders can also be formed by folding under with topstitching.
7. Attach suspenders to the pants.
8. For closure, sew snaps on back of the pants.

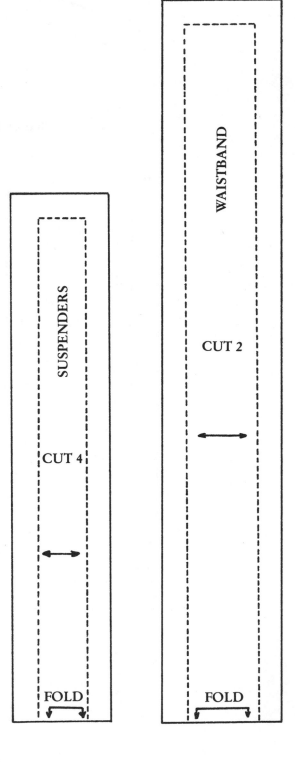

Illus. 82.   Pattern 28 for pants.

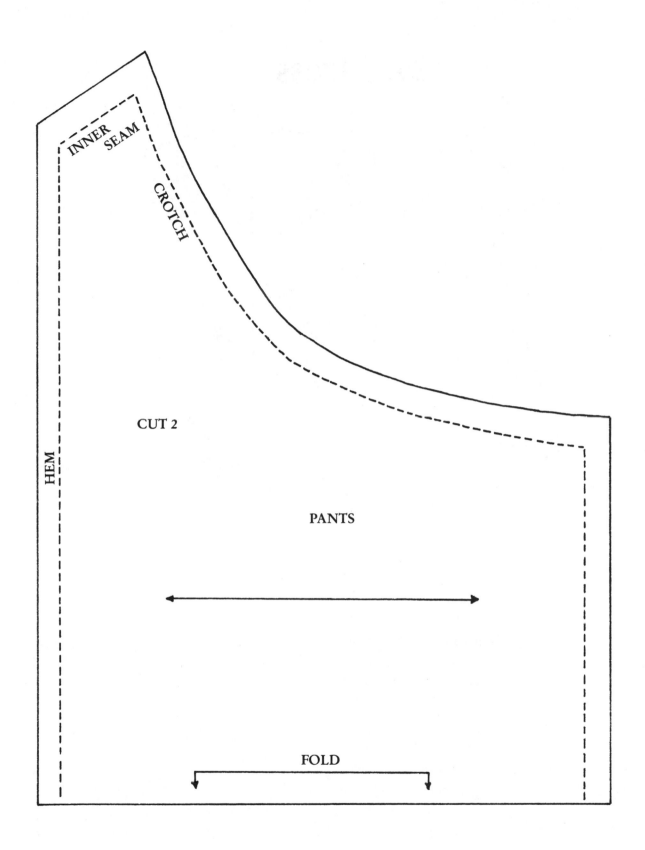

INNER SEAM

CROTCH

HEM

CUT 2

PANTS

FOLD

Illus. 82 (cont.).

29. Dress

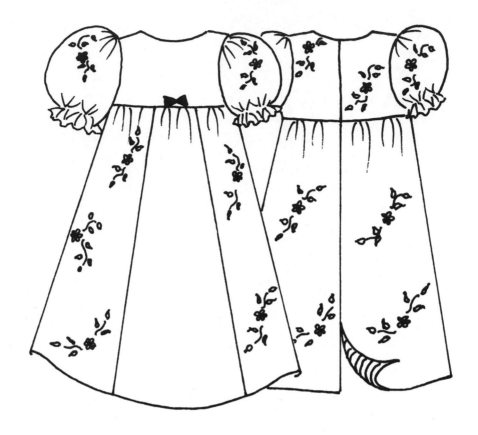

Illus. 83.   Front and back views of Pattern 29.

Supplies
Yardage estimates are based on 45″ width fabric.
¼ yard dress fabric (print)
7″ × 30″ dress fabric (solid)
1 spool thread
¼ yard ⅛″ width elastic

PATTERN 29

This dress fits a fifteen-inch baby-type doll with a cloth body. Dress consists of nine parts. Dress has back opening and elasticized sleeves.

Instructions

1. With right sides together, form the front panels of the skirt: side panels of front skirt and the front-skirt panel.
2. Gather the front-skirt and back-skirt panels.
3. With right sides together, sew the front yoke to the front skirt. In the same way, sew the back yokes to the respective back-skirt panels.
4. With right sides together, join the shoulder seams of the front yoke to the back yokes of the dress; set aside.

5. Gather the sleeves of the dress.
6. At this point, attach the elastic by machine to the sleeves. *Optional:* Trim with lace.
7. With right sides together, sew the sleeves to the dress.
8. With right sides together, sew the side seams of the dress starting from the hem of the dress to the hem of the sleeves.
9. Finish the raw edges by turning under with stitching.
10. *Optional:* Trim the neckline and hem edges with gathered lace.

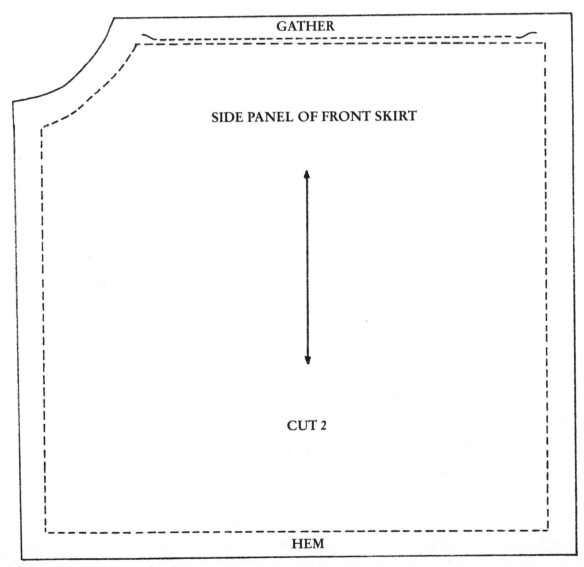

GATHER

SIDE PANEL OF FRONT SKIRT

CUT 2

HEM

Illus. 84. Pattern 29 for dress.

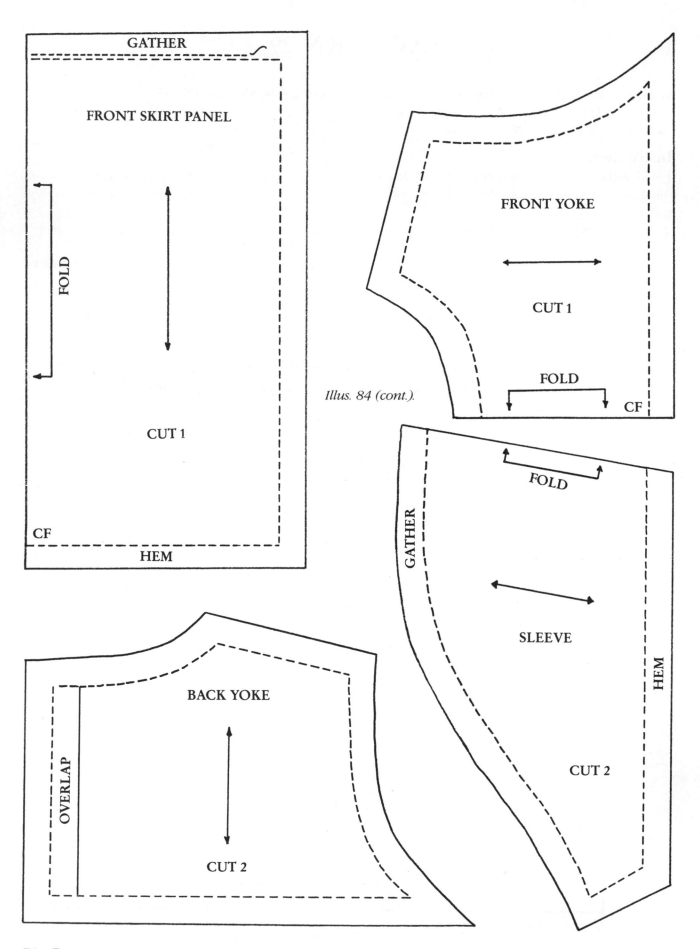

GATHER

FRONT SKIRT PANEL

FOLD

CUT 1

CF

HEM

FRONT YOKE

CUT 1

FOLD

CF

Illus. 84 (cont.).

FOLD

GATHER

SLEEVE

HEM

CUT 2

BACK YOKE

OVERLAP

CUT 2

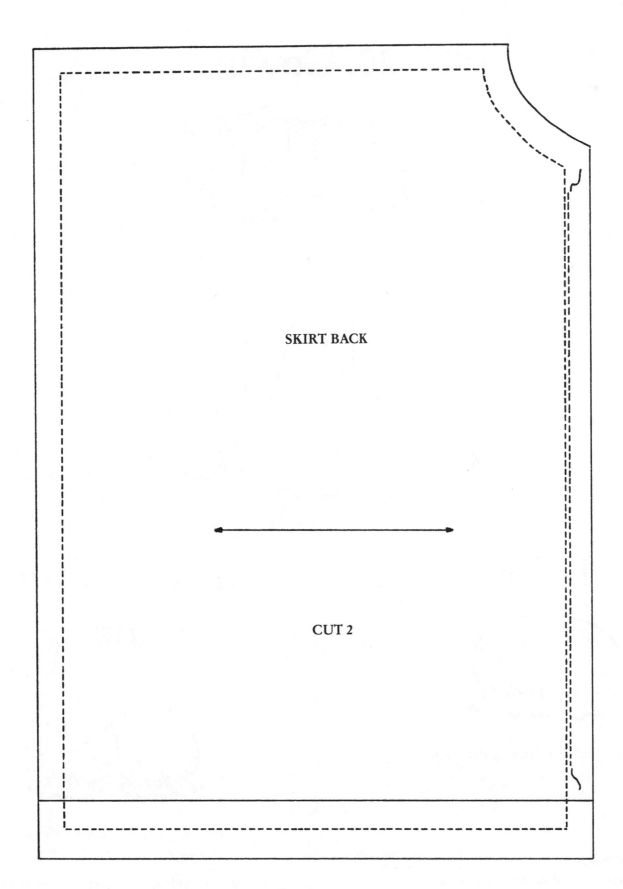

SKIRT BACK

CUT 2

Illus. 84 (cont.).

30. Gown

Illus. 86.   Front and back views of Pattern 30.

31. Cap

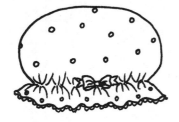

Illus. 85.   Front view of Pattern 31.

32. Pantaloons

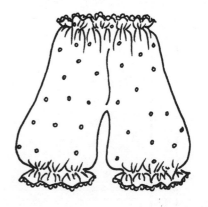

Illus. 87.   Front view of Pattern 32.

Supplies

Yardage based on 45" width fabric.

½ yard dress fabric (combined yardage estimate for Patterns 30, 31 and 32)

4 small snaps for lightweight material

1½ yards double-faced ⅛" width satin ribbon

1½ yards ½" width lace (optional)

1 spool thread

10–14 inches ⅛" width elastic

PATTERN 30

This gown fits a sixteen-inch doll with a girl-type body. It consists of ten parts and has a back opening.

Instructions

1. With right sides together, join two skirt panels to form the front of skirt.
2. Gather front-skirt and back-skirt panels.
3. With right sides together, sew gathered front skirt to the front bodice.
4. In the same way, sew the gathered back-skirt panels to the back-bodice parts.
5. Gather sleeves; set aside.
6. With right sides together, sew shoulder seams of front bodice to the back bodice.
7. With right sides together, sew sleeves to the bodice.
8. With right sides together, sew seams of collar and turn inside out.
9. With right sides together, sew collar into the neckline of the dress.
10. Turn under with stitching, all the raw edges of the dress.
11. *Optional:* Trim sleeves and dress with ribbons and lace.
12. Sew snaps on back for closure.

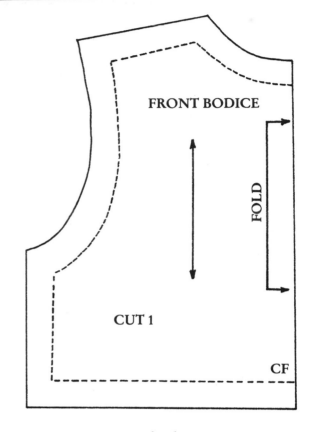

Illus. 88.   Pattern 30 for dress.

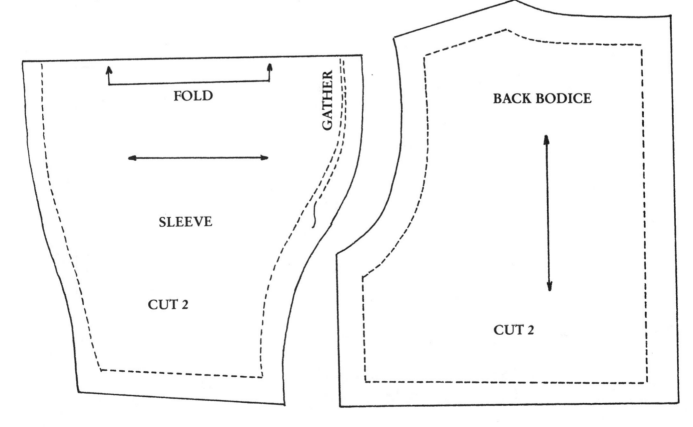

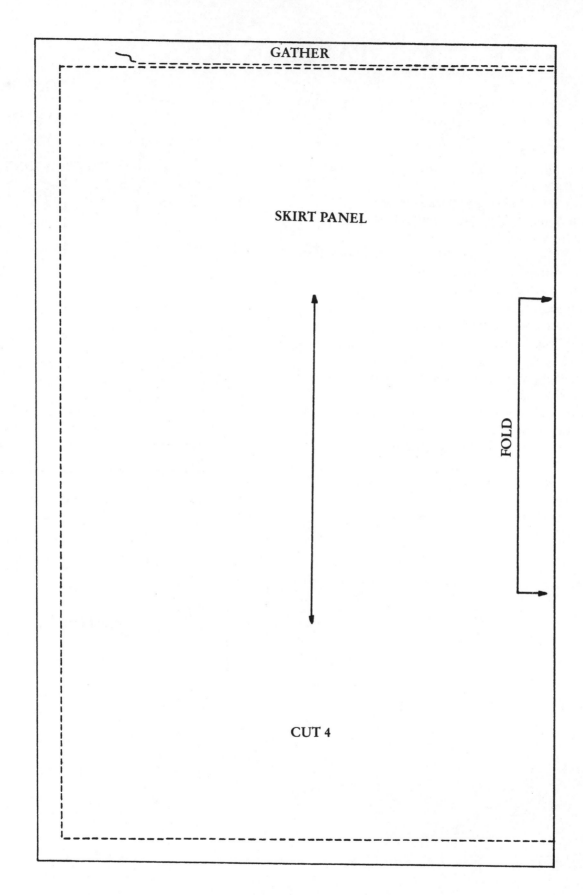

Illus. 88 (cont.).

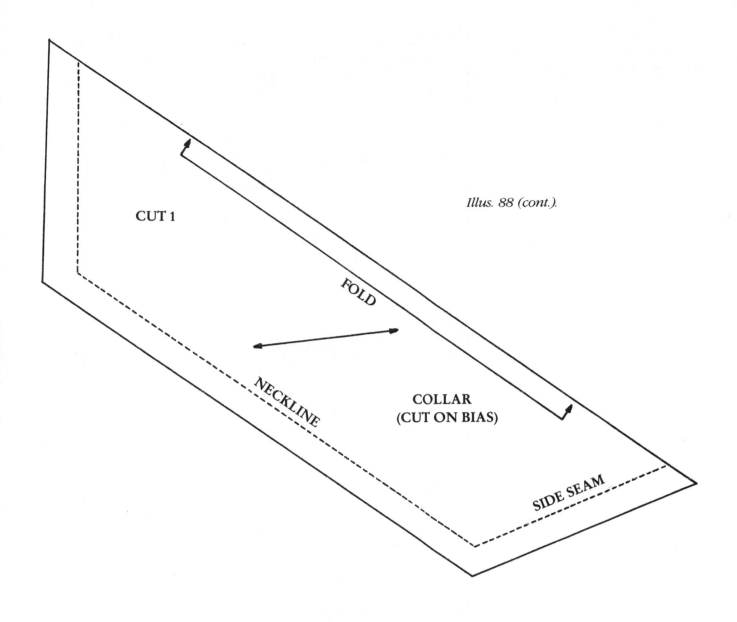

CUT 1

FOLD

NECKLINE

COLLAR
(CUT ON BIAS)

SIDE SEAM

Illus. 88 (cont.).

PATTERN 31

This cap fits a sixteen-inch doll with a girl-type body. The cap fits a head circumference of twelve and a half inches. It consists of only one piece.

Instructions

1. Trim edge with lace. If lace is omitted, turn under with stitching.
2. By machine, sew elastic around the edge about one-half inch away from the hem.

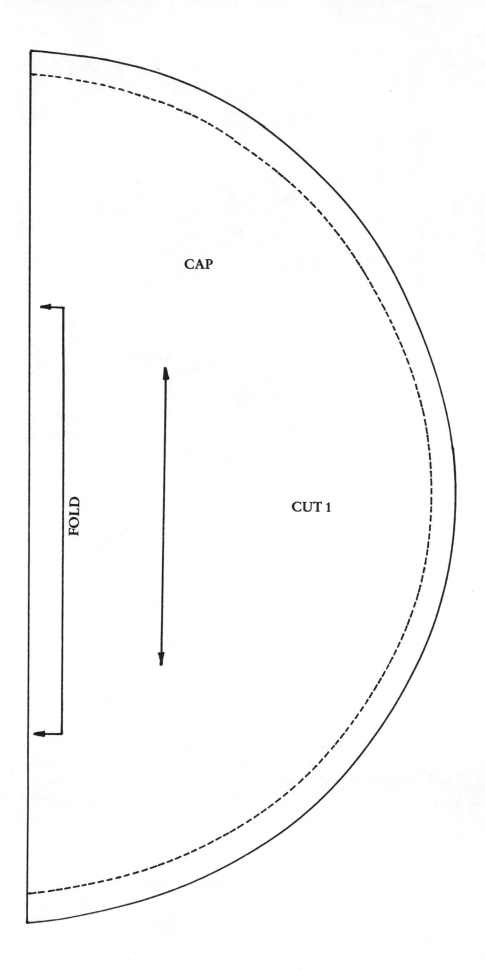

Illus. 89.   Pattern 31.

CAP

FOLD

CUT 1

PATTERN 32

These pantaloons fit a sixteen-inch doll with a girl-type body. Pantaloons consist of four parts.

Instructions

1. With right sides together, sew crotch to form back and front sides of pants (two panels for each side).

2. With right sides together, sew inner seam of front side to back side.
3. With right sides together, sew side seams.
4. By machine, stitch elastic on waistline and leg circumference of pantaloon.

Illus. 90.   Pattern 32 for pantaloons.

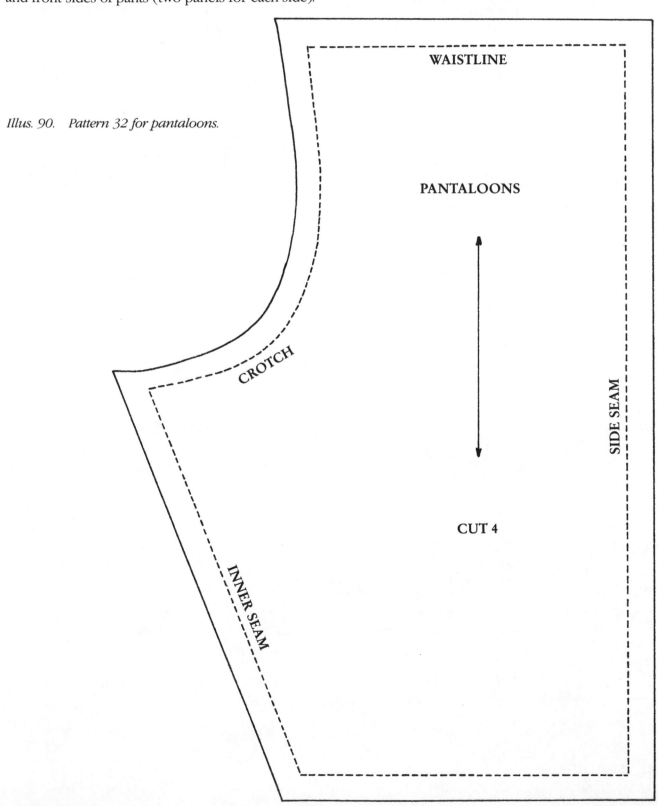

WAISTLINE

PANTALOONS

CROTCH

SIDE SEAM

CUT 4

INNER SEAM

33. Dress

Illus. 91.   Front and back views of Pattern 33.

34. Coat

Illus. 92.   Front and back views of Pattern 34.

35. Pants

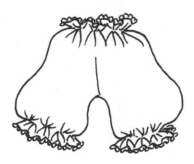

Illus. 93.   Front view of Pattern 35.

36. Bonnet

Illus. 94.   Side view of Pattern 36.

Supplies

Yardage based on 45" width fabric.
*1 yard dress fabric (combined yardage estimate
   for Patterns 33, 34, 35 and 36)*
1 spool thread
3 small snaps for lightweight material
1 yard ¼" width double-faced satin ribbon

6–8 inches ⅛" width elastic
1 yard ½" width lace (optional)
bias tape (optional)

Note: The clothing ensemble is suitable for girl-type
dolls of the 1950's.

PATTERN 33

This dress pattern fits an eighteen-inch doll with a girl-type body. Dress consists of eight pieces and has a back opening.

Instructions

1. Gather front skirt, back-skirt panels and sleeves.
2. With right sides together, sew front skirt to the front yoke. Set aside.
3. With right sides together, sew back-skirt panels to back yokes.

4. Sew sleeves to the assembled bodice.
5. Sew side seams of dress from wrist of sleeves to the hem of the dress.
6. Finish back opening, hem, sleeves and neck by turning under with stitching.
7. For closure, sew snaps on back of dress.
8. *Optional:* Trim edges with lace or bias tape. A one-eighth-inch ribbon may be used to trim around the neckline, sleeves and skirt of dress.

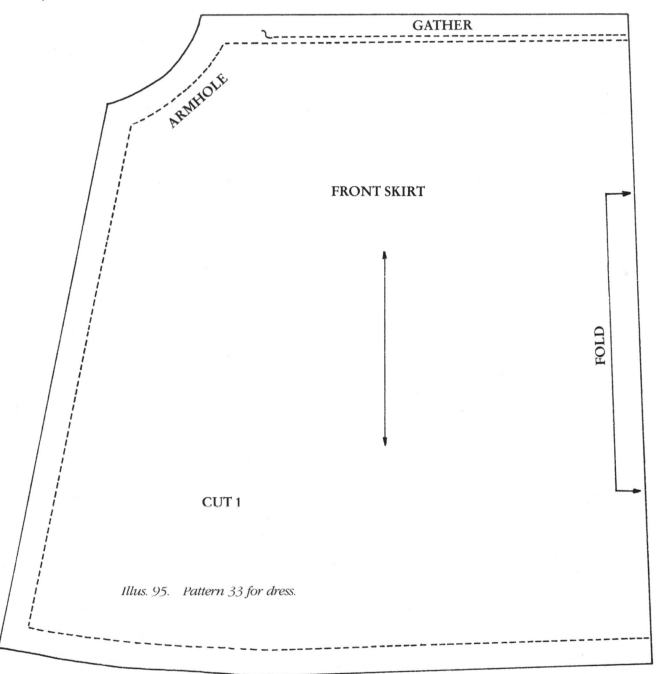

Illus. 95. Pattern 33 for dress.

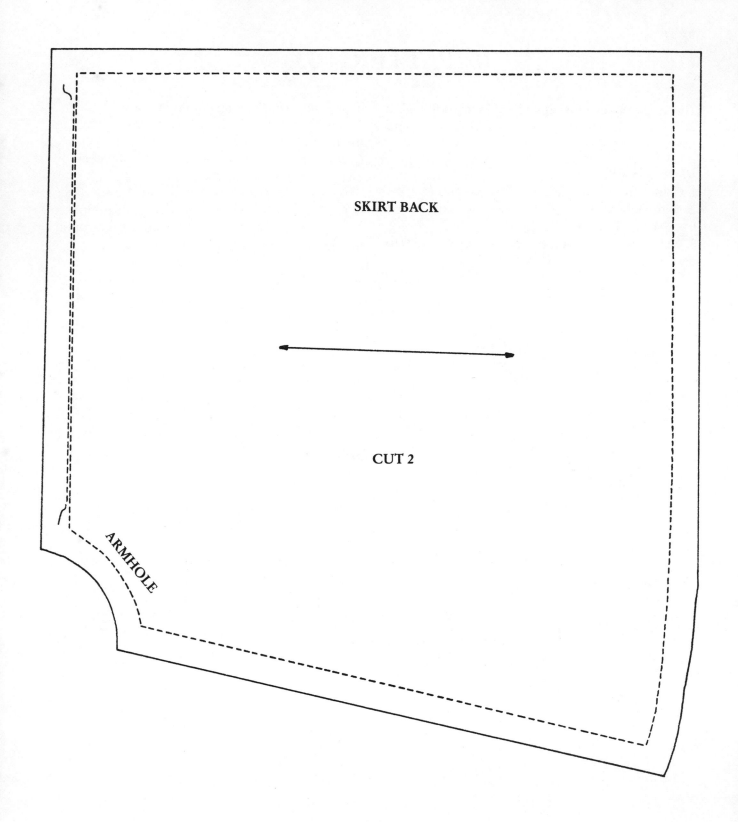

SKIRT BACK

CUT 2

ARMHOLE

Illus. 95 (cont.).

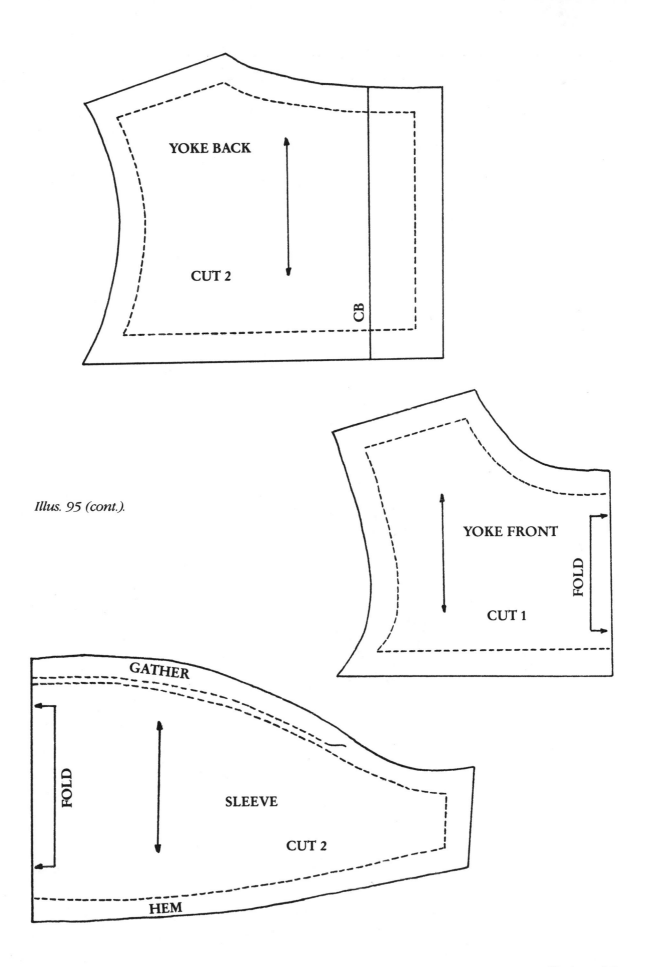

YOKE BACK

CUT 2

CB

Illus. 95 (cont.).

YOKE FRONT

FOLD

CUT 1

GATHER

FOLD

SLEEVE

CUT 2

HEM

PATTERN 34

This coat fits an eighteen-inch doll with a girl-type body. Coat consists of three pattern pieces and has a front opening.

Instructions

1. Baste the pleat on the back of the coat.

2. With right sides together, sew shoulder and side seams of coat front to coat back.
3. Finish the edges of the coat by turning under with stitching.
4. *Optional:* Finish coat edge with bias tape.

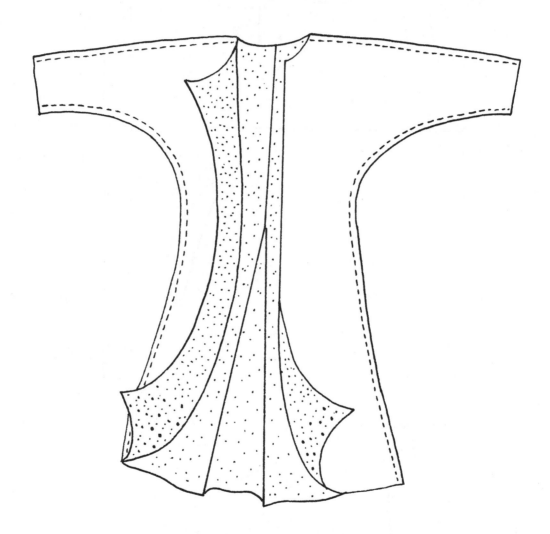

Illus. 96. Front view of coat construction, Pattern 34.

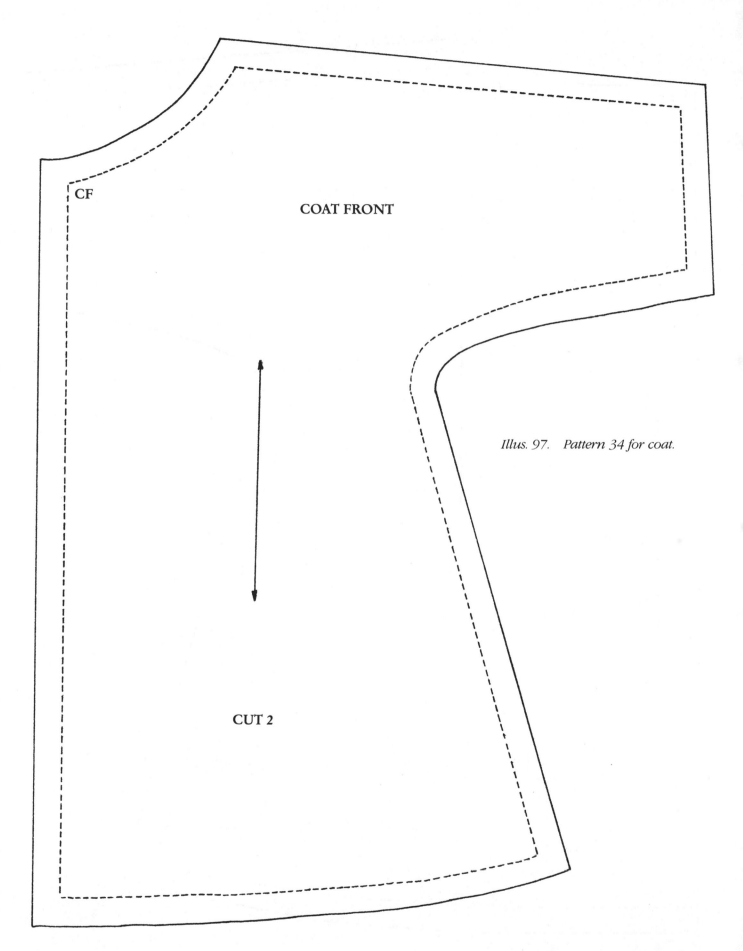

CF

COAT FRONT

Illus. 97.   Pattern 34 for coat.

CUT 2

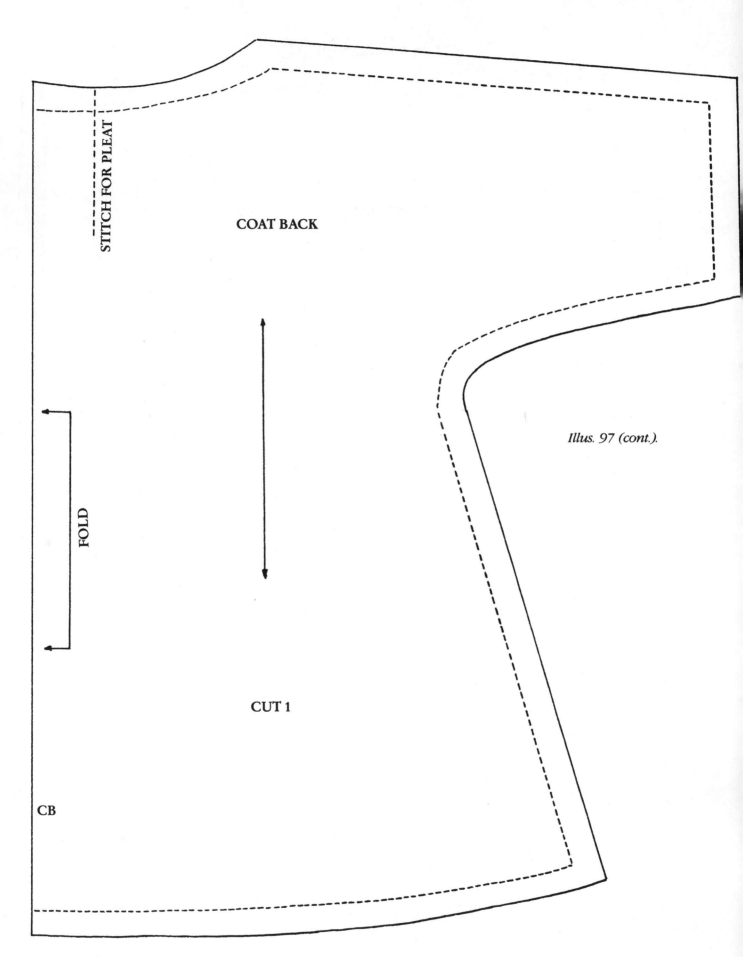

STITCH FOR PLEAT

COAT BACK

FOLD

CUT 1

CB

Illus. 97 (cont.).

PATTERN 35

This undergarment fits an eighteen-inch doll with a girl-type body. The undergarment consists of four parts.

Instructions

1. With right sides together, sew crotch areas to form the front and back of pants.
2. With right sides together, sew side seams and inner seam of pants.
3. Sew elastic on waist and pant-leg circumference by machine.

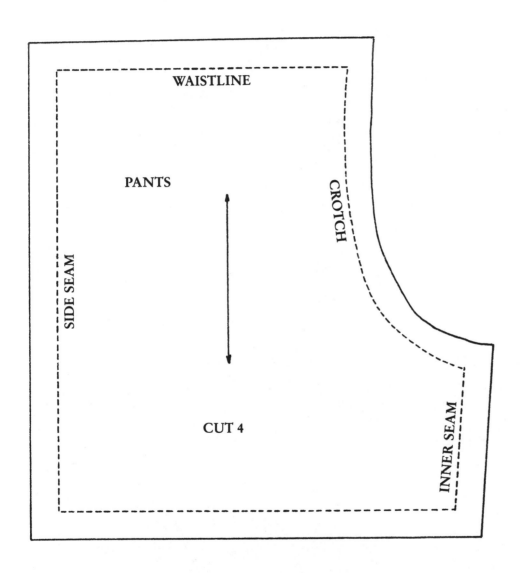

WAISTLINE

PANTS

CROTCH

SIDE SEAM

INNER SEAM

CUT 4

Illus. 98.   Pattern 35 for pants.

PATTERN 36

This bonnet fits an eighteen-inch doll with a head circumference of thirteen inches. Bonnet consists of four pattern parts.

Instruction

1. With right sides together, sew the two parts of the brim together around the front edge. Turn inside out.

2. Topstitch brim around the front edge only.
3. With right sides together, sew back seam of bonnet.
4. With right sides together, sew bonnet to crown.
5. With right sides together, sew bonnet to brim.
6. *Optional:* Sew ribbon ties to the base of the bonnet.

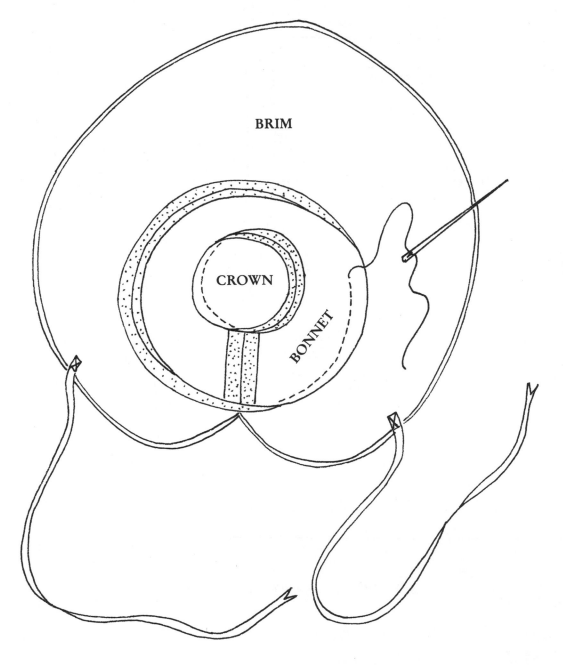

Illus. 99. Inside view of Pattern 36 for hat.

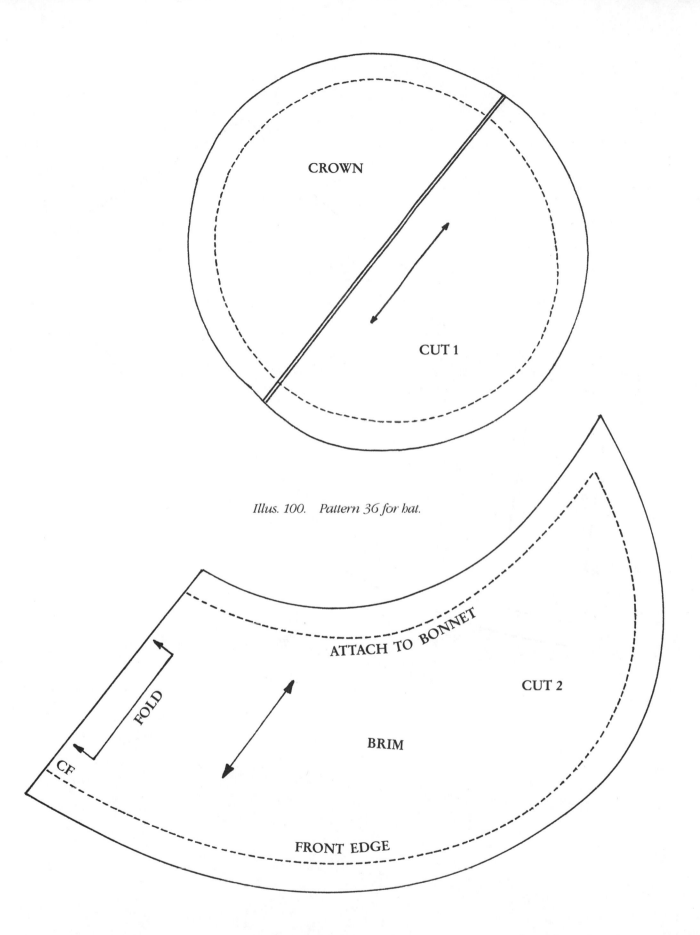

CROWN

CUT 1

Illus. 100.   Pattern 36 for hat.

ATTACH TO BONNET

CUT 2

FOLD

CF

BRIM

FRONT EDGE

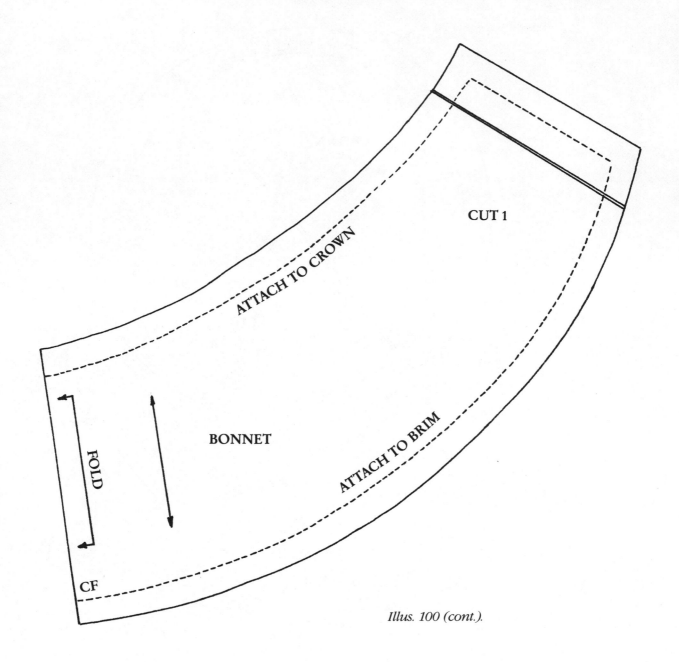

Illus. 100 (cont.).

37. Gown

Illus. 101.   Front and back views of Pattern 37.

38. Pants

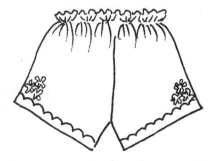

Illus. 102.   Front view of Pattern 38.

Supplies

Yardage based on 45" width fabric.

½ yard dress fabric (combined yardage estimate for Patterns 37 and 38)

5–6 inches ⅛" width elastic
1 spool thread
4 small snaps for lightweight material

PATTERN 37

This dress fits an eighteen-inch doll with a teen-type body. Gown consists of nine parts. Skirt panel may be cut in three pieces: one part for the front of skirt and two for the back of skirt. Gown has back opening.

Instructions

1. With right sides together, sew front-skirt panels (two panels).
2. Gather front-skirt panel, back-skirt panels and sleeves.

3. With right sides together, sew gathered front-skirt panel to the front yoke. In the same fashion, sew back-skirt panels to back yokes.
4. With right sides together, sew the sleeves into the bodice of the garment.
5. With right sides together, sew side seams of the dress from wrist of the sleeves to the hem of the dress.
6. Finish raw edges by turning under with stitching.
7. Sew snaps on back for closure.

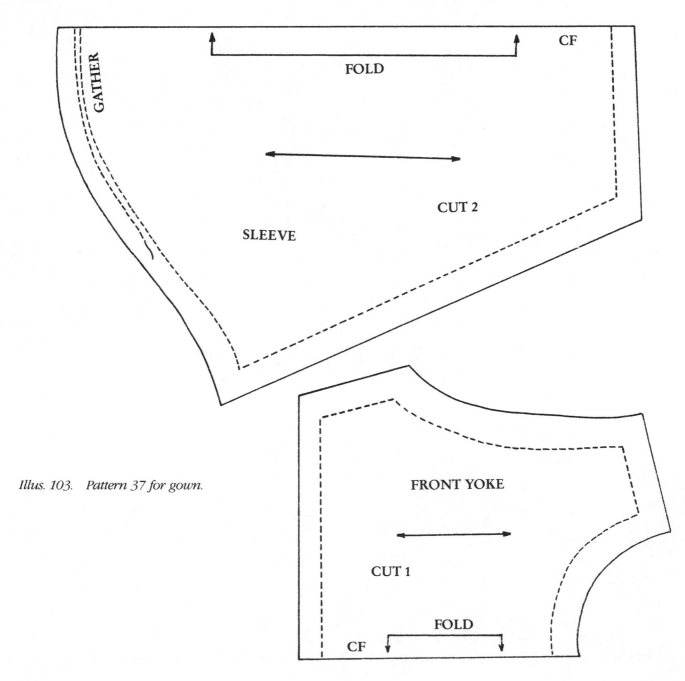

Illus. 103.   Pattern 37 for gown.

96   Dress

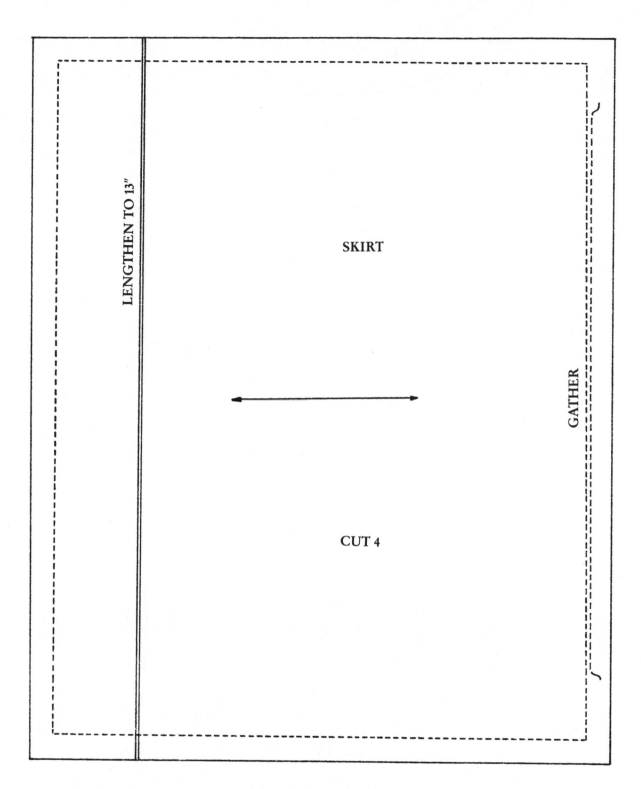

Illus. 103 (cont.).

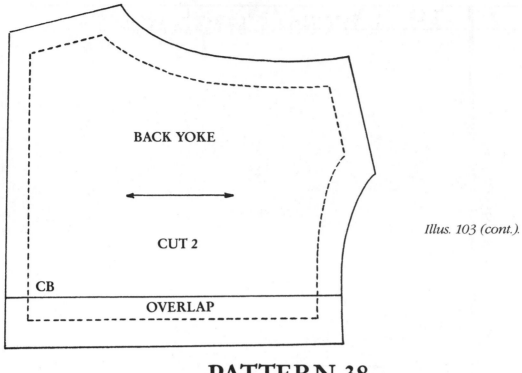

BACK YOKE

CUT 2

CB

OVERLAP

Illus. 103 (cont.).

PATTERN 38

These underpants fit an eighteen-inch doll with a teen-type body. Underpants consist of four parts.

Instructions

1. With right sides together, sew crotch to form the front and back of pants (two panels for each side).

2. With right sides together, sew inner seam of pants.
3. With right sides together, sew side seams.
4. By machine, stitch elastic on waistline and around leg circumference of pants. (Elastic may be omitted on leg circumference.)

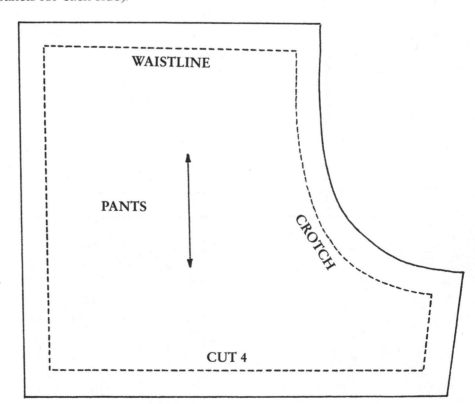

WAISTLINE

PANTS

CROTCH

CUT 4

Illus. 104.   Pattern 38 for pants.

39. Dress/Pinafore

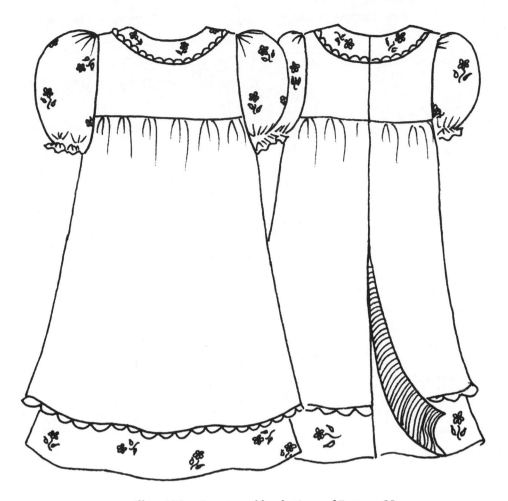

Illus. 105.   Front and back views of Pattern 39.

Supplies

Yardage estimates based on 45" width fabric.
⅓ yard dress fabric
5 small snaps
1 spool thread
⅓ yard ⅛" width elastic
¼ yard dress fabric in solid color

PATTERN 39

This dress/pinafore ensemble fits an eighteen-inch baby-type doll with a cloth body. The dress/pinafore consists of fourteen parts. The pinafore is permanently attached to the dress. Dress/pinafore has back opening.

Instructions

1. With right sides together, join the pinafore front yoke to the pinafore back yokes. Turn under with stitching at the neckline; set aside. *Optional:* Trim neckline with lace.

2. With right sides together, join the shoulder seams of the dress yokes.

3. With right sides together, sew the side seams of the pinafore; set aside.

4. With right sides together, sew the side seams of the skirt.

5. Gather the pinafore skirt and dress skirt together as one piece. The dress skirt should be at the bottom of the layer.

6. With right sides together, join the yokes (pinafore yoke and dress as one piece) and the skirt (pinafore skirt and dress skirt as one piece). Set aside.

7. Gather the sleeves.

8. At this point, trim the sleeves with lace if desired and attach elastic by machine.

9. With right sides together, form the sleeves.

10. With right sides together, sew the sleeves to the dress/pinafore.

11. Finish the raw edges by turning under with stitching.

12. For closure, sew snaps on back of dress/pinafore.

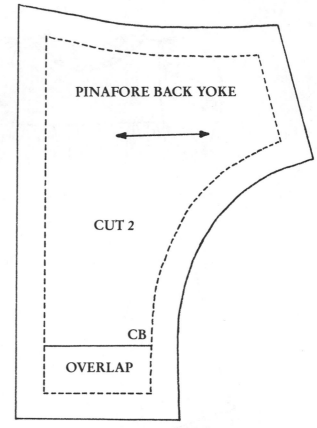

Illus. 106.   Pattern 39 for dress/pinafore.

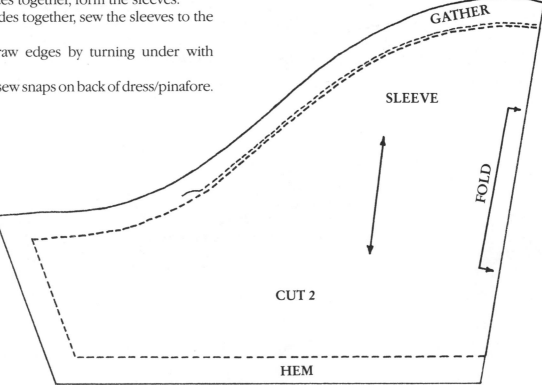

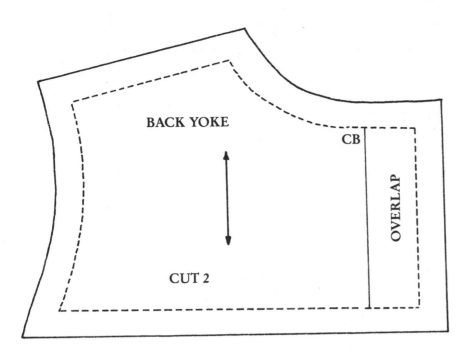

BACK YOKE

CB

OVERLAP

CUT 2

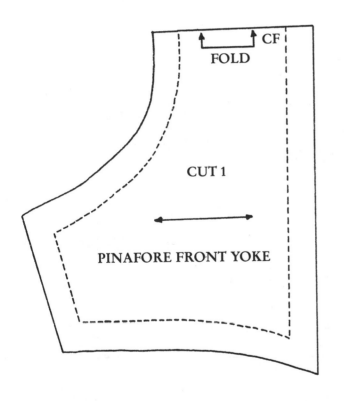

CF

FOLD

CUT 1

PINAFORE FRONT YOKE

Illus. 106 (cont.).

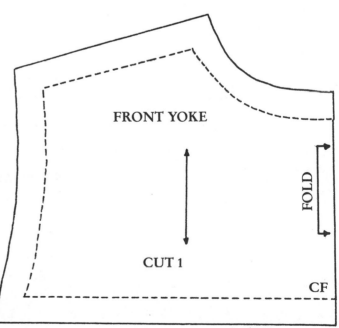

FRONT YOKE

FOLD

CUT 1

CF

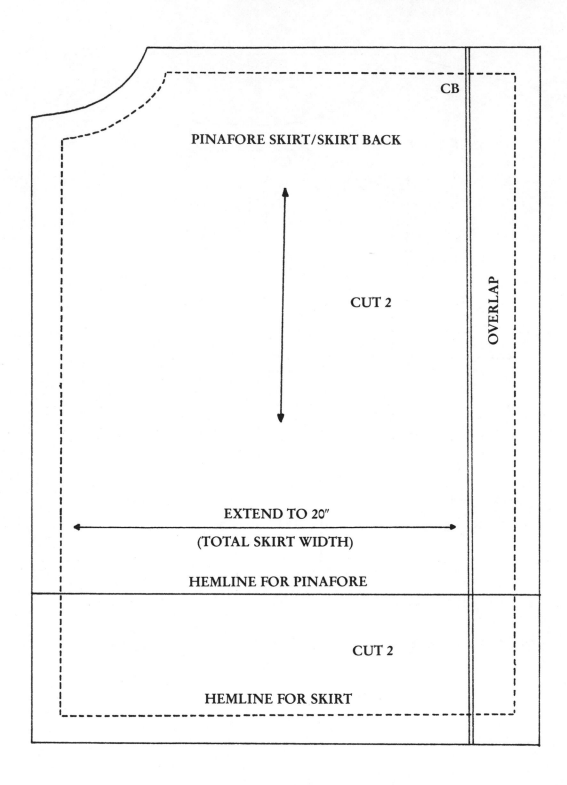

CB

PINAFORE SKIRT/SKIRT BACK

CUT 2

OVERLAP

EXTEND TO 20″

(TOTAL SKIRT WIDTH)

HEMLINE FOR PINAFORE

CUT 2

HEMLINE FOR SKIRT

Illus. 106 (cont.).

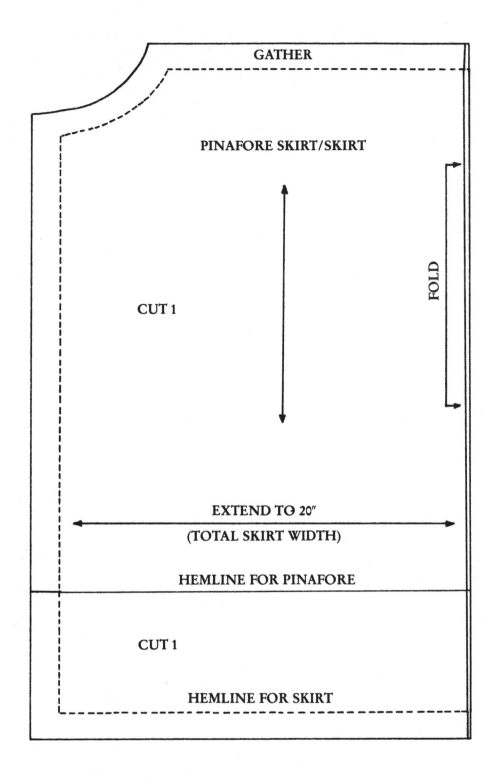

GATHER

PINAFORE SKIRT/SKIRT

FOLD

CUT 1

EXTEND TO 20″

(TOTAL SKIRT WIDTH)

HEMLINE FOR PINAFORE

CUT 1

HEMLINE FOR SKIRT

Illus. 106 (cont.).

40. Bridal Gown

Illus. 107. Front and back views of Pattern 40.

41. Pants

Illus. 109. Front view of Pattern 41.

42. Veil

Supplies

Yardage based on 45" width fabric.

½ yard white satin (combined yardage for
   Patterns 40 and 42)

3 yards 2½" width lace (optional trimming for
   dress and veiling)

1 spool white thread

1 package opaque round beads (optional)

4 snaps for medium-weight material

5 inches ¼" elastic for pants

Illus. 108. Side view of Pattern 42.

PATTERN 40

This bridal gown fits a nineteen-inch lady-type doll. The gown consists of eight parts and has a back opening.

Instructions

1. Baste tucks of front and back bodice.
2. With right sides together, sew front bodice to the front of skirt.
3. In the same way, sew the back-bodice parts to the back-skirt panels.
4. With right sides together, sew shoulder seams of the front bodice to the back bodice.

5. With right sides together, sew sleeves into the bodice.
6. At this point, finish the sleeves by turning under with stitching.
7. With right sides together, sew side seams of gown from wrist of sleeve to the hem of the gown.
8. Finish all remaining edges by turning under with stitching.
9. Decorate gown by trimming with lace, pearl beads and opaque beads.
10. For closure, sew snaps on back of gown.

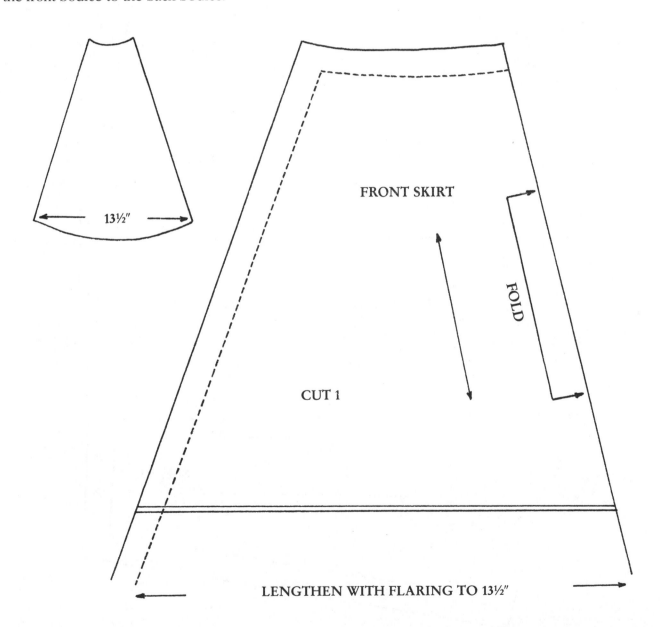

13½"

FRONT SKIRT

FOLD

CUT 1

LENGTHEN WITH FLARING TO 13½"

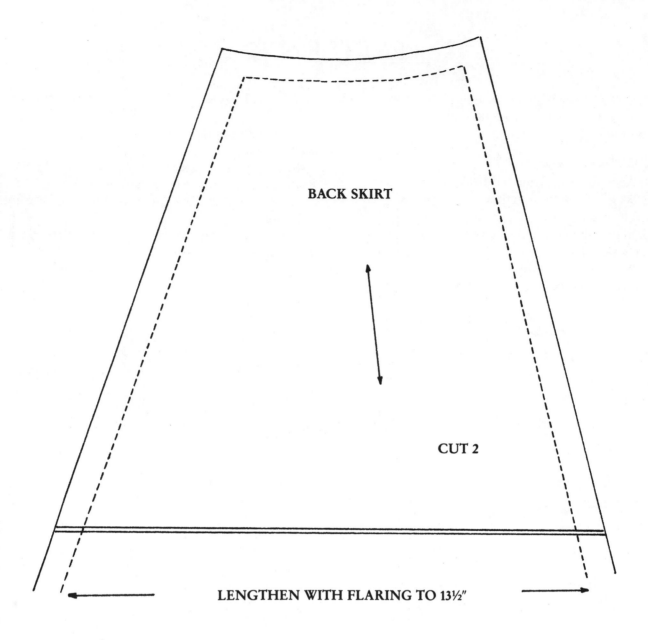

BACK SKIRT

CUT 2

LENGTHEN WITH FLARING TO 13½"

Illus. 110 (cont.).

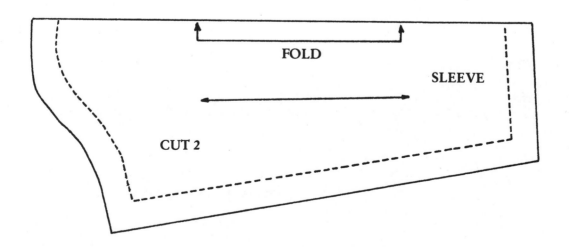

FOLD

SLEEVE

CUT 2

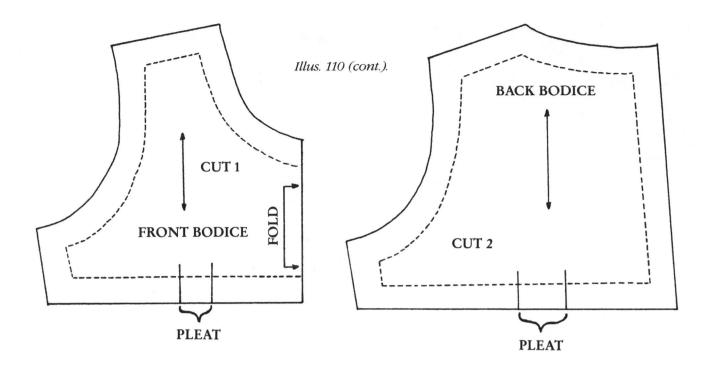

Illus. 110 (cont.).

CUT 1

FRONT BODICE

FOLD

PLEAT

BACK BODICE

CUT 2

PLEAT

PATTERN 41

These pants fit a nineteen-inch doll with a lady-type body. Pants consist of four parts.

Instructions

1. With right sides together, sew crotch of two sets of pants to form the front and back of pants.
2. With right sides together, sew side seams.
3. With right sides together, sew inner seam of pants.
4. Attach elastic on waistline and hem of pants by machine.

Illus. 111.   Pattern 41 for pants.

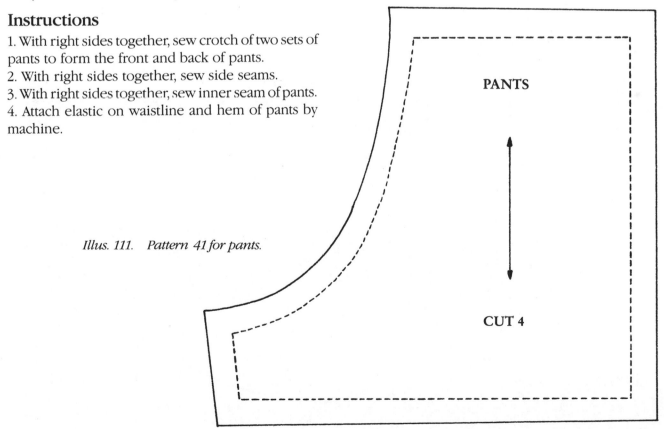

PANTS

CUT 4

PATTERN 42

This veil fits a nineteen-inch doll with a lady-type body. Veil will fit any head size. The veil consists only of one part with the addition of lace trim on the crown.

Instructions

1. Draw a full circle with a thirty-inch diameter.
2. Fold the veil, about ten inches from the edge to form the first layer of the veil. Gather at this point.
3. Trim gathered area with gathered lace or artificial flowers.
4. *Optional:* Trim around the edge of the veil with a 2½ inch width lace.

Illus. 112.   Schematic diagram of veil for Pattern 42.

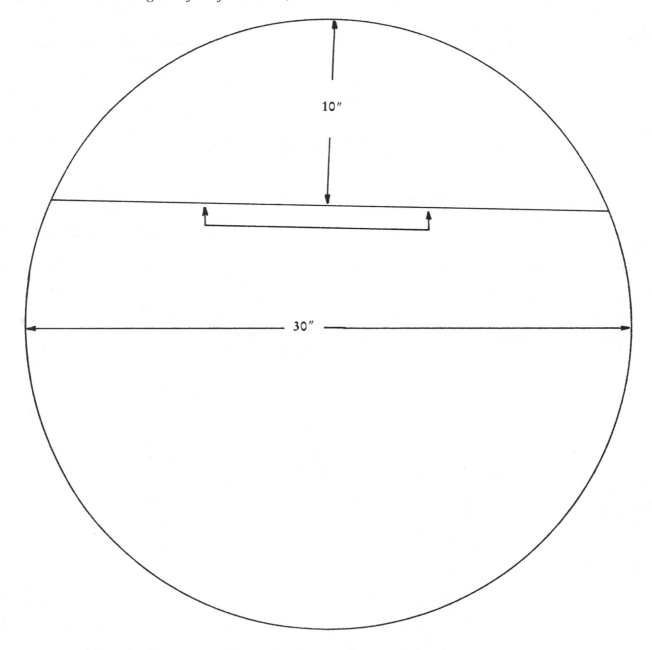

10"

30"

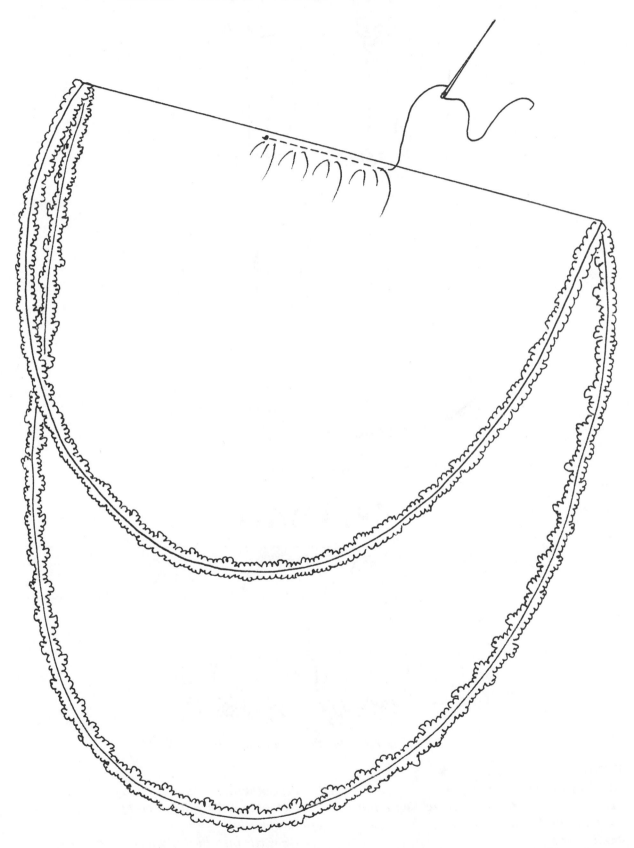

43. Gown

Illus. 114.   Front and back views of Pattern 43.

44. Pants

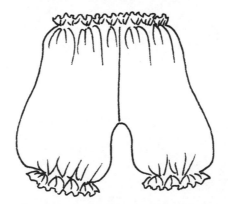

Illus. 115.   Front view of Pattern 44.

Supplies

Yardage based on 45" width fabric.

½ yard dress fabric (combined yardage estimate
   for Patterns 43 and 44)

1 spool thread

3–4 inches ⅛" width elastic

1 spool thread

1 spool metallic gold thread for running stitches
   (optional)

1½ yards metallic gold trim (optional)

4 small snaps for lightweight material

PATTERN 43

This gown fits a twenty-inch doll with a lady-type body. It consists of thirteen parts and has a back opening.

Instructions

1. With right sides together, sew front-skirt panel (two skirt panels).
2. Gather sewn front panels and two back panels.
3. With right sides together, sew gathered front-skirt panel to the front yoke. In the same way, sew gathered back-skirt panels to back yokes, leaving the center-back seam open.
4. With right sides together, sew shoulder seams of the front yoke to the back yokes.
5. With right sides together, sew two sets of collars. Turn inside out and topstitch collar pieces.
6. With right sides together, sew collar into the neckline of the dress.
7. Gather sleeves.
8. With right sides together, sew the sleeves into the bodice.
9. With right sides together, sew side seams of the dress, starting from the wrist of the sleeves to the hem of the dress.
10. Turn under with stitching all the raw edges of the dress.
11. Sew snaps on back for closure.
12. *Optional:* Trim dress with gold trim and embroidery. (Running stitch is applied parallel to the gold trim.)

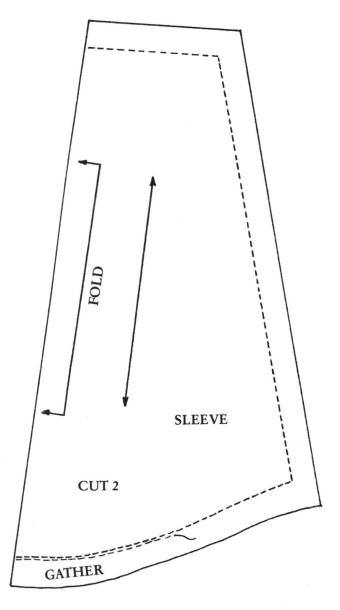

Illus. 116. Pattern 43 for gown.

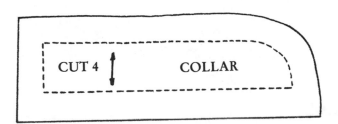

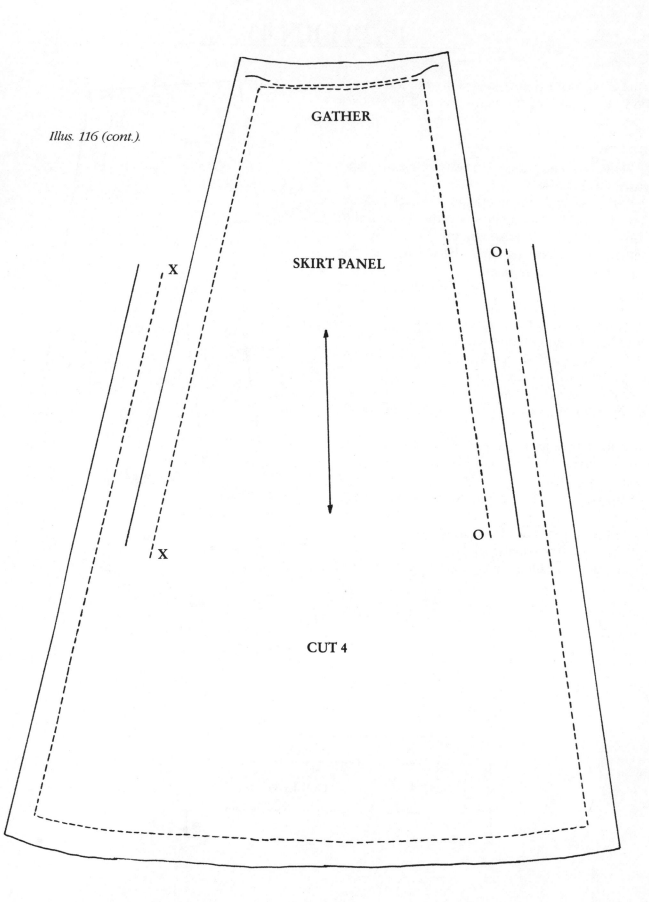

Illus. 116 (cont.).

GATHER

SKIRT PANEL

X

O

X

O

CUT 4

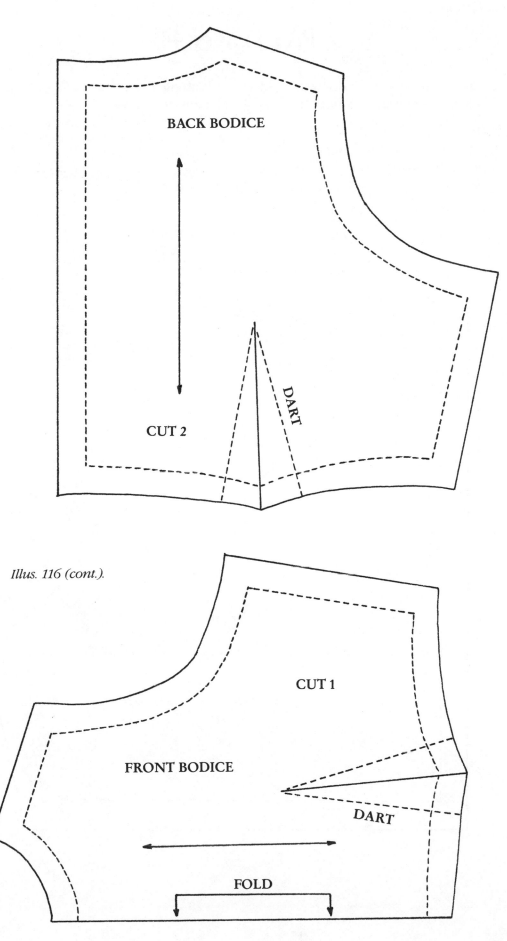

BACK BODICE

DART

CUT 2

Illus. 116 (cont.).

CUT 1

FRONT BODICE

DART

FOLD

PATTERN 44

These underpants fit a twenty-inch doll with a lady-type body. Underpants consist of four parts.

Instructions

1. With right sides together, sew crotch of pants to form the front and back sides (two panels for each side).

2. With right sides together, sew inner seam of front of pants to the back of pants.
3. With right sides together, sew side seams of pants.
4. Machine-stitch elastic on waistline and leg circumference of pants.
5. *Optional:* Trim pants with lace.

Illus. 117.   Pattern 44 for underpants.

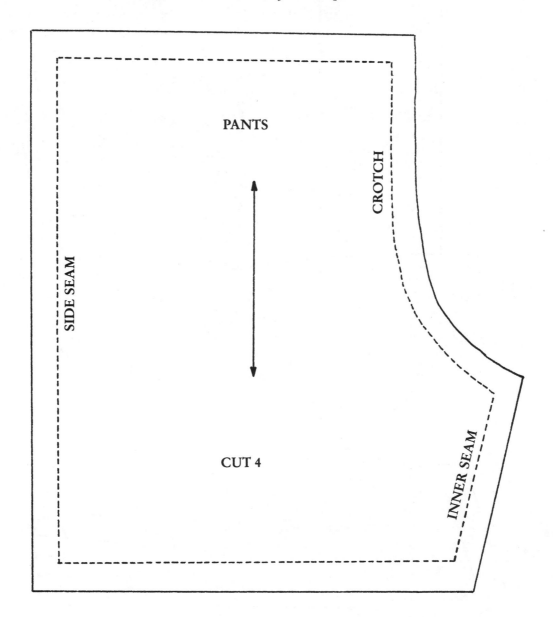

PANTS

SIDE SEAM

CROTCH

INNER SEAM

CUT 4

45. Dress

Illus. 119.   Front and back views of Pattern 45.

46. Bonnet

Illus. 118.   Front view of Pattern 46.

47. Pants

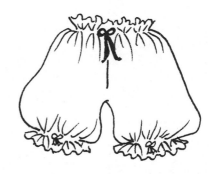

Illus. 120.   Front view of Pattern 47.

Supplies
Yardage based on 45″ width fabric.
*¾ yard dress fabric (yardage estimate for Patterns
    45, 46 and 47)*
1 spool thread
3 small snaps for lightweight material
6–8 inches ⅛″ width elastic
½ yard ¼″ width lace (optional)
artificial flowers and feathers (optional)

PATTERN 45

This dress fits a twenty-inch doll with a lady-type body. Dress consists of eleven parts. The skirt may be cut in one continuous pattern or divided into two panels. Dress has a back opening.

Instructions

1. Sew front darts of front bodice.
2. With right sides together, sew shoulder seams of front bodice to the back bodice.
3. Gather sleeves.
4. Sew sleeves to bodice. Set aside.
5. Sew all six panels of the skirt, leaving one side of the first and last panel unsewn. Unsewn sides will be centered to the middle of the back bodice for the dress opening.
6. Gather skirt.
7. With right sides together, sew skirt to the bodice.
8. With right sides together, sew side seams of dress.
9. To finish the dress, turn under with stitching around the raw edges.
10. Sew snaps on back of dress for closure.
11. *Optional:* Trim dress with lace as illustrated.

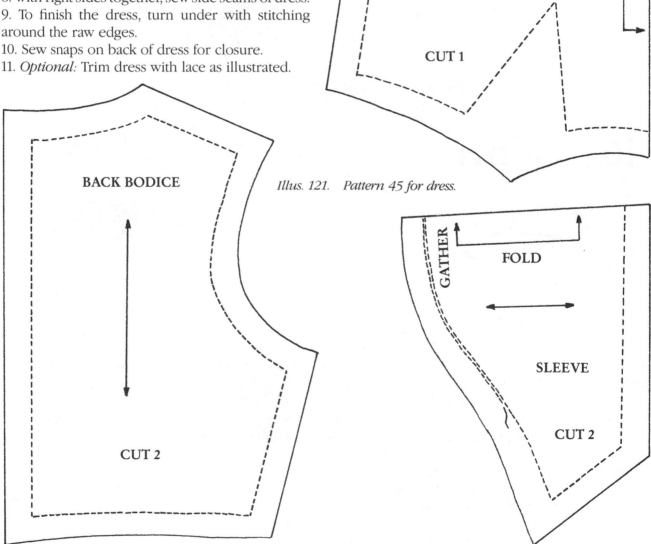

Illus. 121.   Pattern 45 for dress.

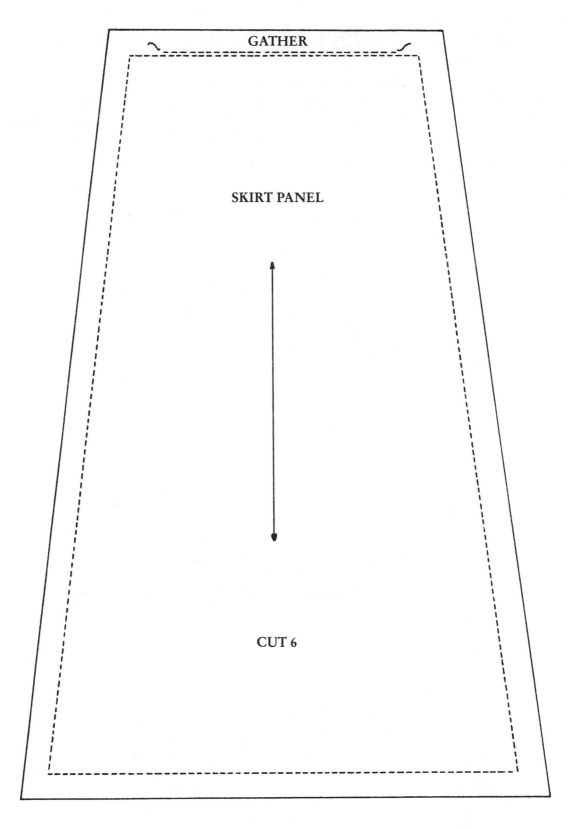

GATHER

SKIRT PANEL

CUT 6

Illus. 121 (cont.).

PATTERN 46

This bonnet fits a twenty-inch doll with a head circumference of thirteen inches. Bonnet consists of six pattern parts.

Instructions

1. Sew all sides; set aside.

2. With right sides together, sew the two parts of brim together. Turn inside out.
3. Topstitch the edge of the brim towards the front.
4. With right sides together, sew.
5. *Optional:* Trim bonnet with artificial flowers and feathers.

Illus. 122.   Pattern 46 for bonnet.

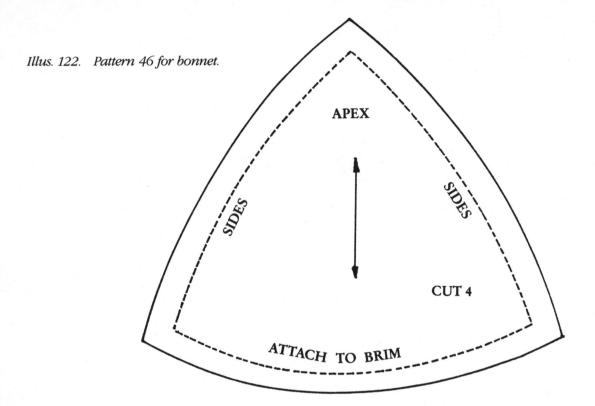

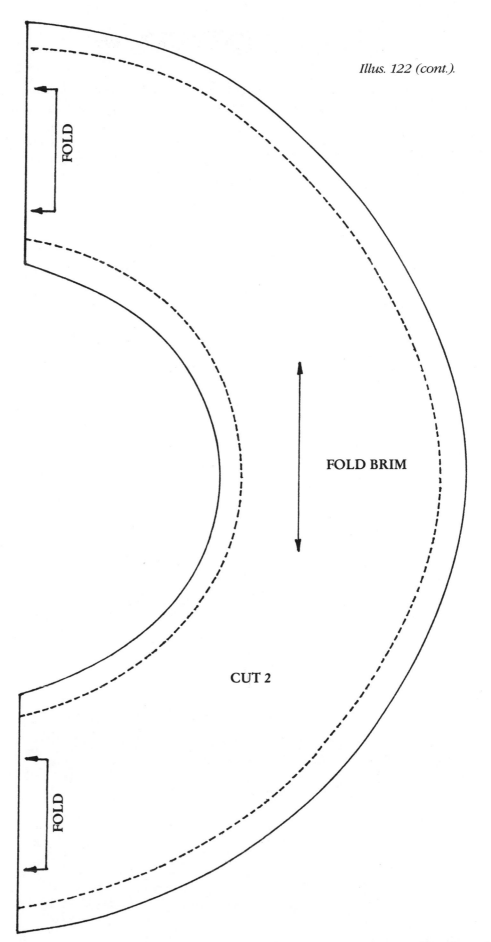

FOLD

FOLD BRIM

CUT 2

FOLD

PATTERN 47

These pants fit a twenty-inch doll with lady-type body. Pants consist of four pattern pieces.

Instructions

1. With right sides together, sew crotch to form the front side and back side of pants.

2. With right sides together, sew inner seams and side seams of front to back of pants.
3. Trim waistline and around pant leg with lace.
4. By machine, sew elastic around waistline and leg circumference of pants.

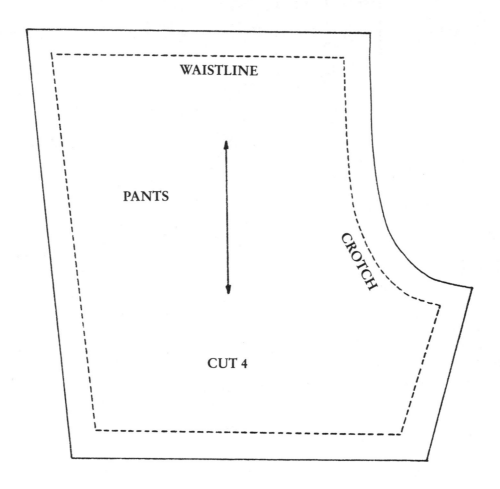

Illus. 123. Pattern 47 for pants.

48. Jacket

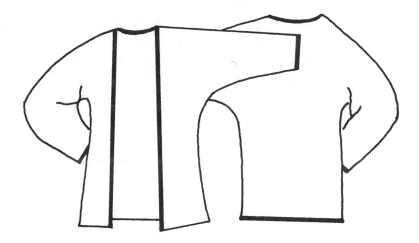

Illus. 124.   Front and back views of Pattern 48.

49. Pants

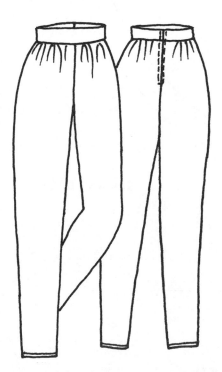

Illus. 125.   Front and back views of Pattern 49.

50. Blouse

Illus. 126.   Front and back views of Pattern 50.

Supplies
Yardage based on 45″ width fabric.
*¼ yard lightweight woven suiting fabric
    (combined yardage for Patterns 48 and 49)*
5 small snaps
1 package single-fold bias tape (optional)
*⅛ yard lightweight woven fabric (yardage
    estimate for Pattern 50)*
1 spool thread

PATTERN 48

This jacket pattern fits a twelve-inch fashion-type doll. It consists of three parts.

Instructions

1. With right sides together, join the shoulder seams of the front of jacket to the back sections of the jacket.

2. At this point, finish the hem of the sleeves by turning under with stitching or finishing with bias tape.

3. With right sides together, sew the side seams of the jacket.

4. Finish the raw edges of the jacket by turning under with stitching or by finishing with bias tape.

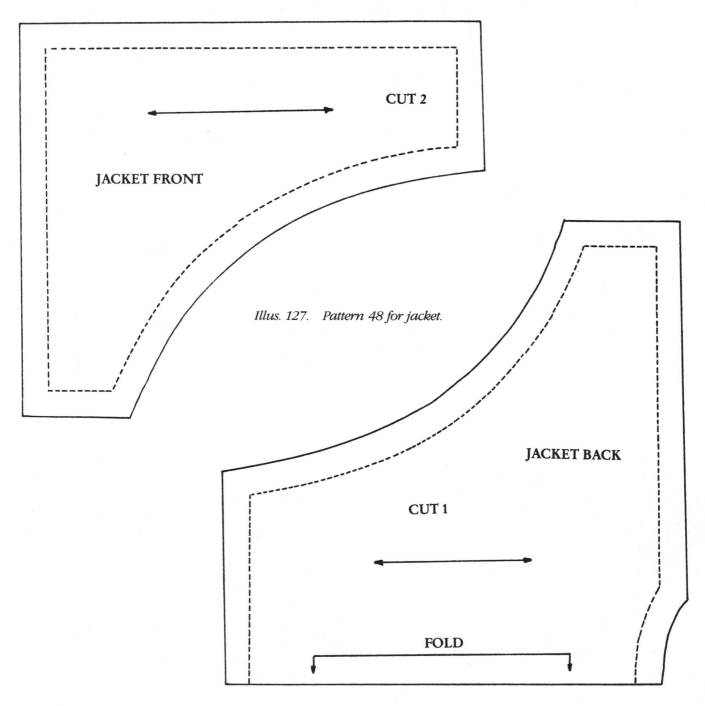

JACKET FRONT

CUT 2

Illus. 127. Pattern 48 for jacket.

JACKET BACK

CUT 1

FOLD

PATTERN 49

This trousers pattern fits a twelve-inch fashion-type doll. The trousers consist of four parts and have a back opening.

Instructions

1. With right sides together, sew the crotch of the pants together leaving two-thirds of the back section unsewn for the opening.
2. At this point, hem the pants by turning under with stitching.
3. Gather the waist of the pants to fit the waistband. Set aside.
4. With right sides together, sew the side seams of the waistband; turn inside out.
5. With right sides together, sew the waistband to the pants. Allow extension for attachment of the snaps.
6. With right sides together, sew the inseam of the pants.
7. Sew snaps on back of pants for closure.

Illus. 128. Pattern 49 for trousers.

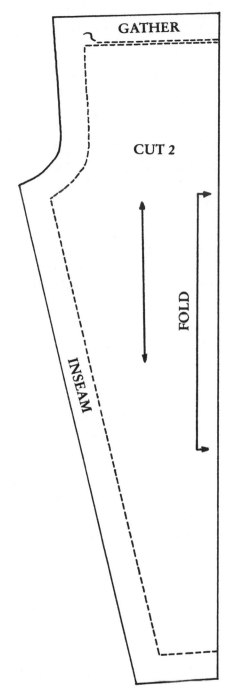

PATTERN 50

This blouse pattern fits a twelve-inch fashion-type doll. Blouse consists of four parts and has a back opening.

Instructions

1. With right sides together, join the front of the blouse to the back sections. Set aside.
2. With right sides together, form the collar by sewing the side seams. Turn inside out and set aside.
3. Gather the neckline of the blouse to fit the collar.
4. With right sides together, sew the collar to the blouse.
5. At this point, finish the armholes by turning under with stitching.
6. With right sides together, sew the side seams of the blouse.
7. Finish the raw edges by turning under with stitching.
8. Sew snaps on back for closure.

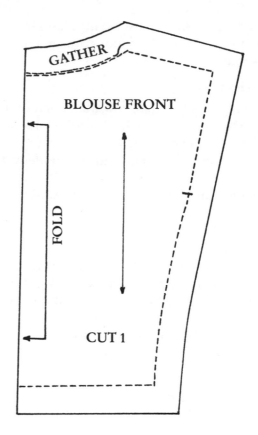

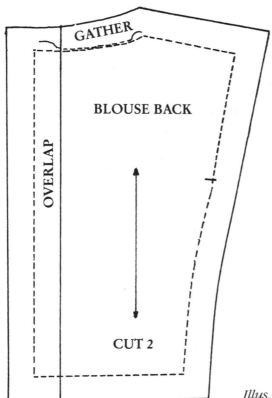

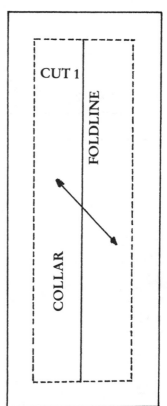

Illus. 129.   Pattern 50 for blouse.

51. Shirt

Illus. 130.   Front and back views of Pattern 51.

52. Jogging Pants

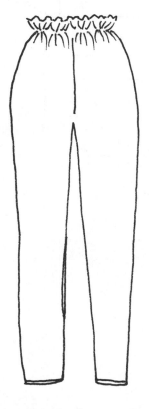

Supplies
Yardage based on 45″ width fabric.

¼ yard lightweight knit fabric (combined yardage for Patterns 51 and 52)

¼ yard ¼″ wide satin ribbon or inset material (optional)

3 inches ⅛″ wide elastic

3 small snaps

1 spool thread

Illus. 131.   Front and back views of Pattern 52.

PATTERN 51

This shirt fits a twelve-inch fashion-type doll. Shirt primarily consists of three parts. Striped inset is optional and may be replaced with ribbons (¼ inch width), topstitched in place.

Instructions

1. Topstitch ribbons in front of shirt if desired. Omit step for plain effect.
2. With right sides together, sew the shoulder of the front shirt to the back-shirt panels.
3. At this point, hem the sleeves of the shirt.
4. With right sides together, sew the side seams of the shirt.
5. Finish the raw edges with zigzag or overlock stitches.
6. Sew snaps on back for closure.

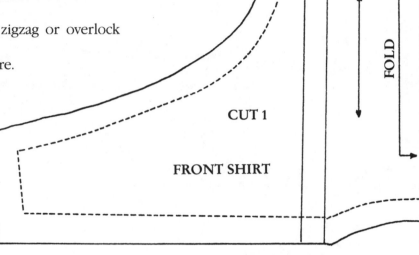

Illus. 132. Pattern 51 for shirt.

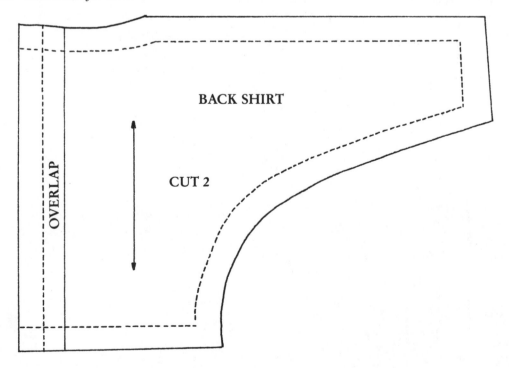

PATTERN 52

These jogging pants fit a twelve-inch fashion-type doll. Jogging pants consist only of two parts and are elasticized at the waist.

Instructions

1. With right sides together, sew the crotch of the pants.
2. At this point, hem the pants with zigzag or overlock stitches.
3. With right sides together, sew the inseam of pants.
4. Machine-stitch elastic to the waist of pants.

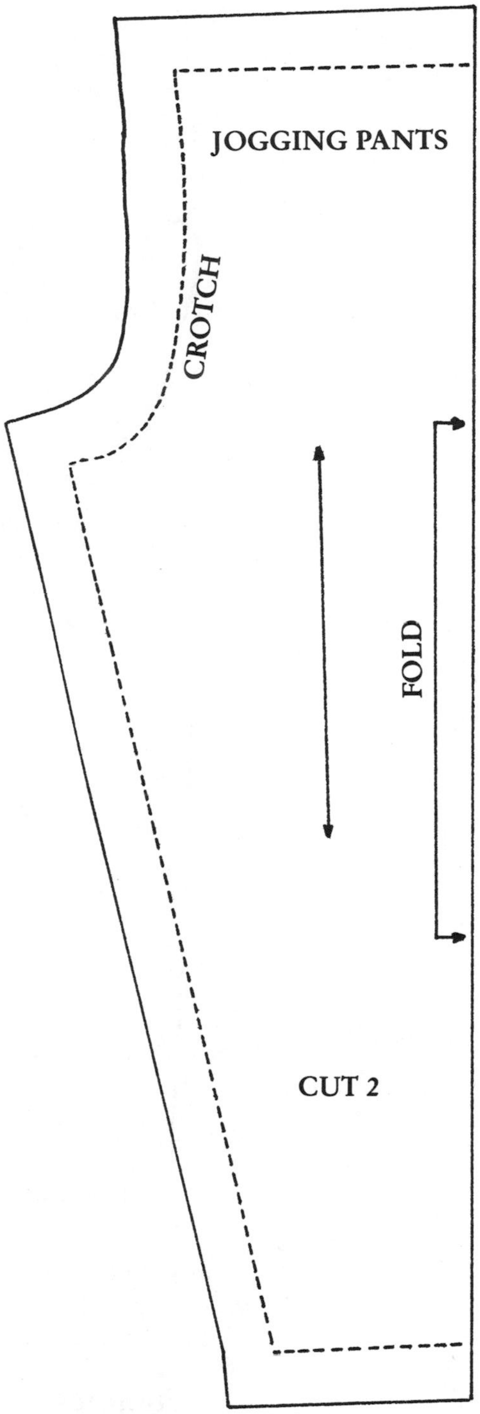

Illus. 133.   Pattern 52 for jogging pants.

JOGGING PANTS

CROTCH

FOLD

CUT 2

53. Gown

54. Stole

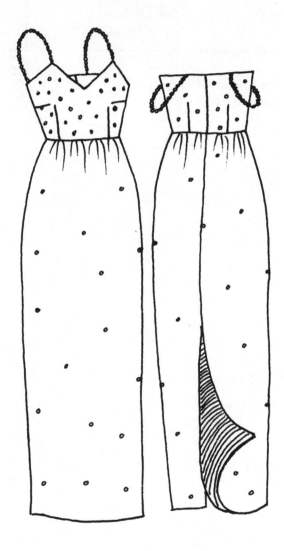

Illus. 134.   Front and back views of Pattern 53.

Supplies
Yardage based on 45″ width fabric.
¼ yard lightweight dress material
6 × 6 square-inch fake fur
2 packages bugle beads (optional)
1 package small pearl beads (optional)
5 small snaps
1 spool thread

PATTERN 53

This gown fits a twelve-inch fashion-type doll. Gown consists of six parts and has a back opening.

Instructions

1. With right sides together, sew the darts of the front and back bodice; set aside.
2. Gather the front- and back-skirt panels.
3. With right sides together, sew the front bodice to the front skirt. In the same way, sew the back-bodice sections to the respective skirt panels.
4. With right sides together, sew the side seams of the gown.
5. Finish the raw edges by turning under with stitching.
6. Sew snaps on back for closure.
7. Embellish the gown with sequins and beads.
8. *Optional:* String beads for shoulder straps.

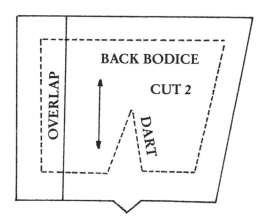

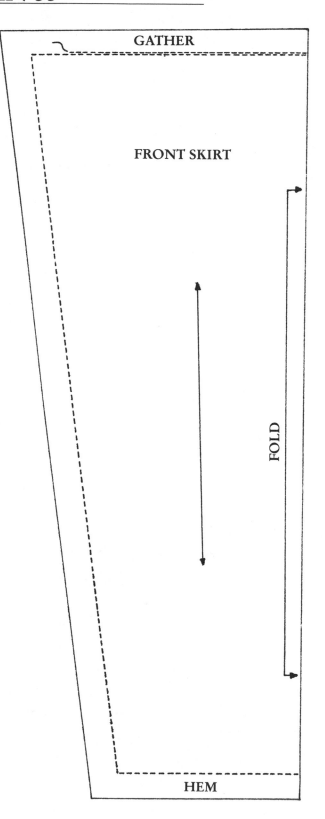

Illus. 135. Pattern 53 for gown.

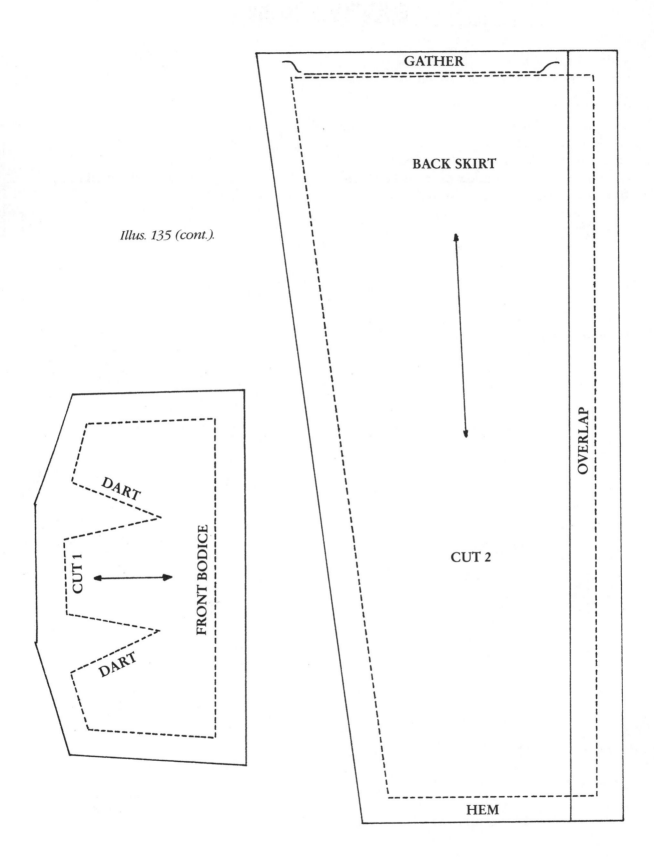

Illus. 135 (cont.).

GATHER

BACK SKIRT

OVERLAP

CUT 2

HEM

DART

CUT 1

FRONT BODICE

DART

PATTERN 54

This stole fits a twelve-inch fashion-type doll. Stole does not require sewing unless a lining is desired.

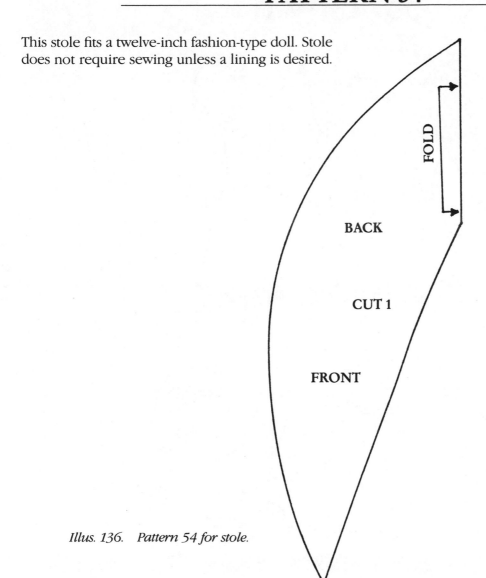

Illus. 136.   Pattern 54 for stole.

55. Gown

Illus. 137.   Front and back views of Pattern 55.

Supplies

Yardage estimates are based on 45" width fabric.

⅓ yard lightweight satin fabric
2½ yards ¼" wide trimming lace (optional)
¼ yard floral Venetian lace—cut to scatter
  (optional)
1 package small pearl beads (optional)
1 package transparent beads (optional)
¼ yard veiling (optional)
1 spool thread
6 small snaps
3 inches ⅛" wide elastic

PATTERN 55

This wedding gown fits a twelve-inch fashion-type doll. Gown consists of eleven parts and has a back opening.

Instructions

1. With right sides together, sew the darts of the front- and back-bodice sections.
2. With right sides together, sew the side seams of the front bodice to the back-bodice sections; set aside.
3. At this point, attach the lace to the cuffs and proceed to attach the elastic.
4. With right sides together, form the sleeves of the gown.
5. With right sides together, sew the sleeves to the bodice of the gown.
6. Finish the neckline with zigzag or overlock stitching.
7. Gather the top edge of the sleeves to fit the neckline of the doll. For a perfect fit, you will need the doll to measure the fullness of the sleeve gathers.
8. Staystitch the neckline area to prevent the sleeve gathers from shifting.
9. Gather the skirt tiers: gather tier 1 to fit the waist of the bodice, gather tier 2 to fit the hem of tier 1, and gather tier 3 to fit the hem of tier 2.
10. With right sides together, sew the skirt tiers in their respective order: tier 1 to tier 2 and tier 2 to tier 3.
11. With right sides together, sew the skirt to the bodice of the gown.
12. For closure, sew snaps on back of gown.
13. *Optional:* Attach scattered lace with beading for embellishment.

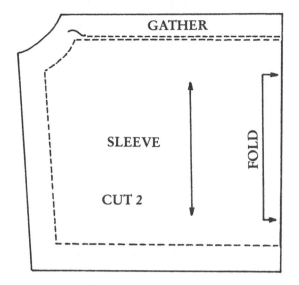

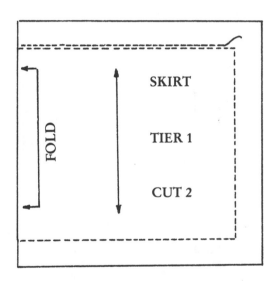

Illus. 138. Pattern 55 for bridal gown.

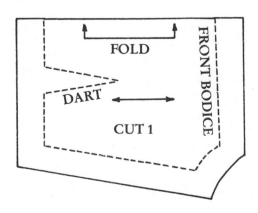

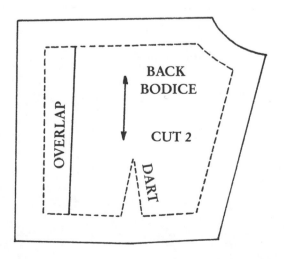

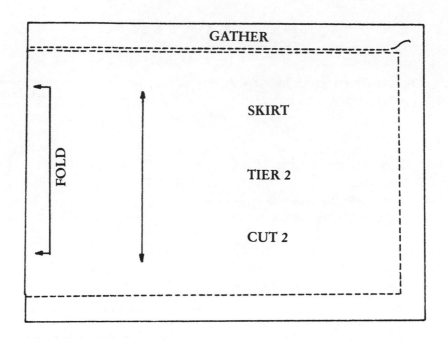

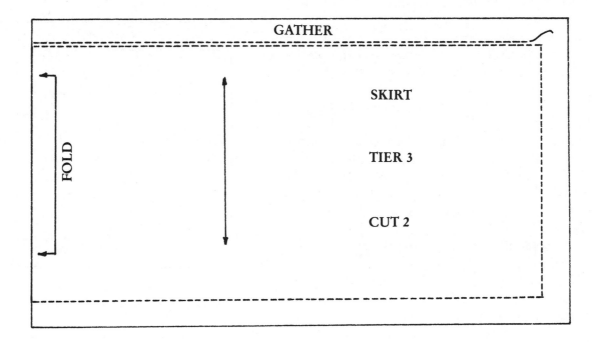

Illus. 138 (cont.).

56. Jacket

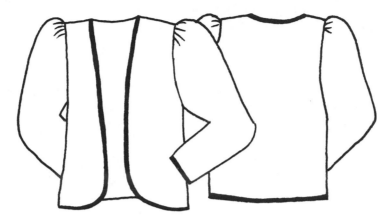

Illus. 139. Front and back views of Pattern 56.

57. Skirt

Illus. 140. Front and back views of Pattern 57.

58. Blouse

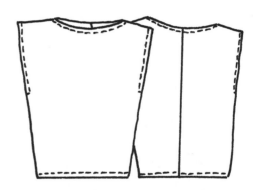

Illus. 141. Front and back views of Pattern 58.

Supplies

Yardage based on 45″ width fabric.

¼ yard lightweight woven suiting fabric (combined yardage for Patterns 56 and 57)

7 small snaps

1 package single-fold bias tape (optional)

1 spool thread

⅛ yard lightweight woven fabric or lace material (Pattern 58)

PATTERN 56

This jacket pattern fits a twelve-inch fashion-type doll. Jacket consists of five parts.

Instructions

1. With right sides together, sew the shoulder seams of the front sections of jacket to the back; set aside.
2. At this point, finish the hem of the sleeves by turning under with stitching.
3. Gather the sleeves of the jacket.
4. With right sides together, sew the sleeves to the bodice of the jacket.
5. With right sides together, sew the side seams of the jacket. Start from the hem of the sleeves to the hem of the jacket.
6. Finish the raw edges of the jacket by turning under with stitching or finishing with bias tape.

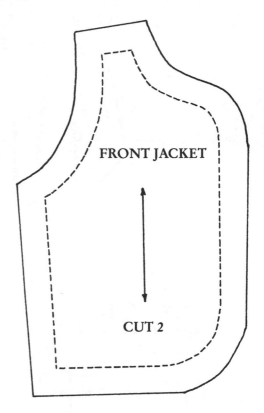

FRONT JACKET

CUT 2

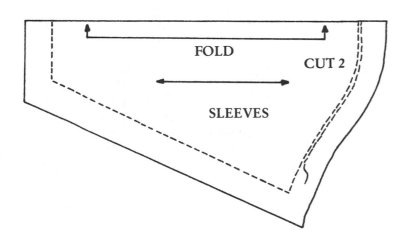

FOLD

CUT 2

SLEEVES

Illus. 142.   Pattern 56 for jacket.

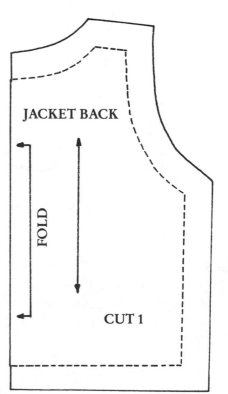

JACKET BACK

FOLD

CUT 1

PATTERN 57

This skirt fits a twelve-inch lady-type fashion doll. Skirt is pleated in the front and has back closure and consists of five parts.

Instructions

1. With right sides together, sew the darts of the skirt.
2. With right sides together, form the pleat of the front skirt. Press to set the pleats flat.
3. With right sides together, sew the side seams of the skirt.
4. Form the waistband by sewing its side seams. Turn inside out.
5. With right sides together, sew the waistband to the skirt.
6. Finish the raw edges by turning under with stitching.
7. For closure, sew snaps on the back of skirt.

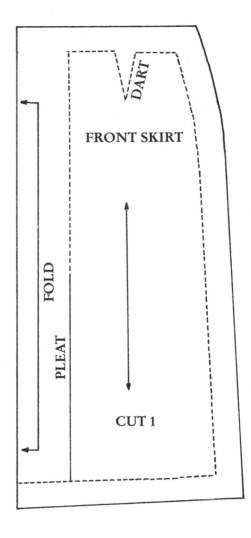

Illus. 143. Pattern 57 for skirt.

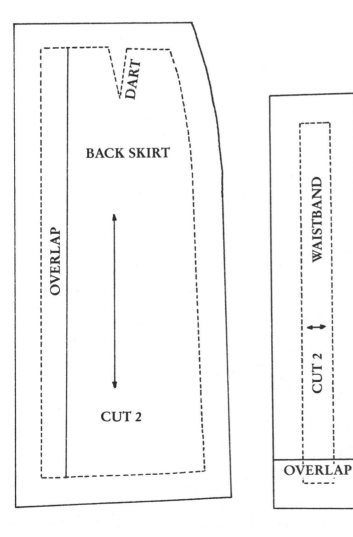

PATTERN 58

This blouse fits a twelve-inch fashion-type doll. Blouse consists of three parts and has a back opening.

Instructions

1. With right sides together, sew the shoulder seams of the blouse.
2. At this point, finish the armhole by turning under with stitching.
3. With right sides together, sew the side seams of the blouse.
4. Finish the neckline, hem of blouse and raw edges of the back by turning under with stitching.
5. For closure, sew snaps on back.

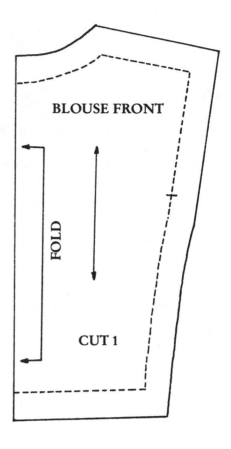

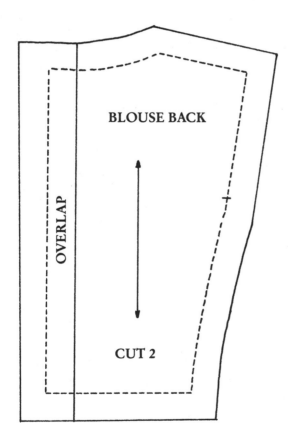

Illus. 144. Pattern 58 for blouse.

59. Robe

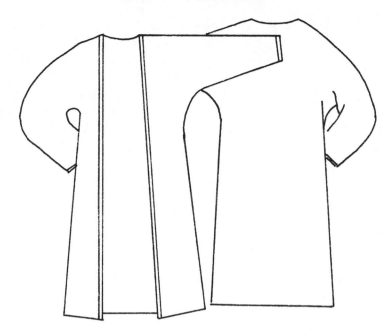

Illus. 145.   Front and back views of Pattern 59.

60. Swimsuit

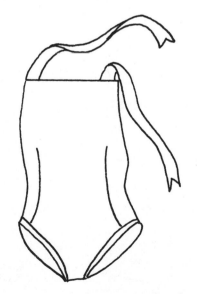

Illus. 146.   Front view of Pattern 60.

Supplies

Yardage based on 45" width fabric.

¼ yard lightweight knit fabric (combined yardage for Patterns 59 and 60)

9"w × 5"l lightweight knit fabric (Pattern 60 only)

¼ yard ¼" wide satin ribbon

1 package single-fold bias tape (optional)

1 small snap

1 spool thread

PATTERN 59

This robe fits a twelve-inch fashion-type doll. The robe consist of three parts.

Instructions

1. With right sides together, sew the shoulder seams of the robe.
2. Hem the sleeves of the robe by turning under with stitching or by finishing the edges with contrasting bias tape.
3. With right sides together, sew the side seams of the robe.
4. Finish the remaining edges by turning under with stitching or finish the raw edges with contrasting bias tape.

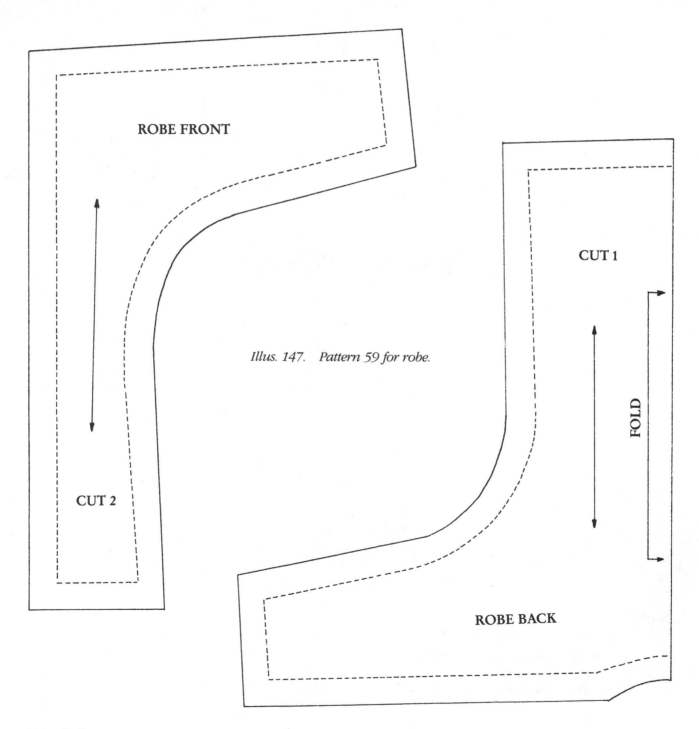

Illus. 147. Pattern 59 for robe.

ROBE FRONT

CUT 2

CUT 1

FOLD

ROBE BACK

PATTERN 60

This swimsuit fits a twelve-inch fashion-type doll. Swimsuit consists only of one part. Swimsuit has back opening.

Instructions

1. With right sides together, sew the darts (A to B).
2. With right sides together, sew the center-back seam of the swimsuit. To facilitate a wider back opening, stitching may be carried to a halfway point only.
3. At this point, hem the leg opening of the swimsuit by turning under with stitching.
4. With right sides together, sew the inseam of the swimsuit.
5. Attach ribbon ties or self-made strap to the front of the swimsuit.

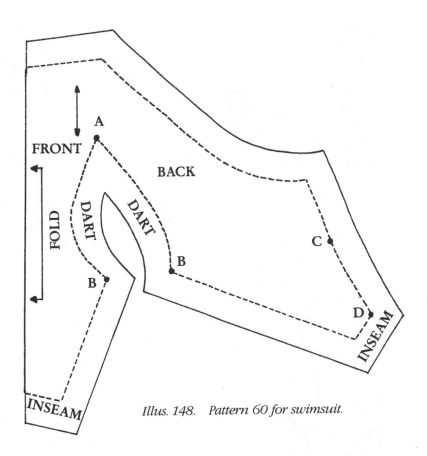

Illus. 148.   Pattern 60 for swimsuit.

1)

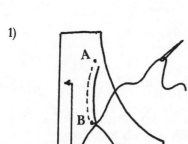

4)

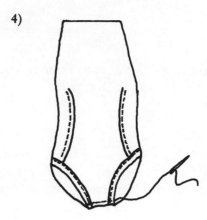

2)

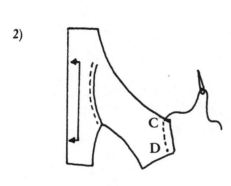

5)

Illus. 149.   Construction steps 1,2,3,4 and 5 for Pattern 60.

3)

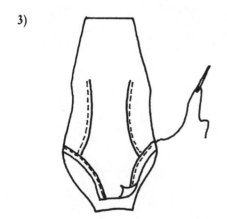

61. Bridal Gown

Illus. 150. Front and back views of Pattern 61.

Supplies

Yardage based on 45" width fabric.
¼ yard lightweight satin woven fabric
⅛ yard sheer fabric
1 package small pearl beads (optional)
½ yard Venetian floral lace—cut to scatter
*   (optional)*
1¼ yard ¼" wide lace trimming (optional)
6 small snaps
1 spool thread
3 inches ⅛" wide elastic

PATTERN 61

This bridal gown fits a twelve-inch fashion-type doll. It consists of eleven parts and has a back opening.

Instructions

1. Turn under with stitching the neckline of the satin lining of the bodice (front and back sections).
2. Using wide hand-stitching, baste the front bodice of the lining material to the sheer front-bodice material. In the same way, follow this step for the back bodice.
3. With right sides together, sew the darts.
4. At this point, attach the elastic and lace to the cuff of the sleeves.
5. Gather the sleeves; set aside.
6. With right sides together, sew the shoulder seams.
7. At this point, attach lace to the neckline.
8. Place slight gathers to the neckline. Staystitch in place. You may need the doll for fitting.
9. Gather the front-skirt panel and do the same with the back-skirt panels.
10. With right sides together, sew the front skirt to the front bodice of the gown and follow the same step for the back panels of the gown.
11. With right sides together, sew the sleeves to the bodice of the gown.
12. With right sides together, sew the side seams of the gown from the hem of the gown to the hem of the sleeves.
13. Finish the raw edges by turning under with stitching.
14. *Optional:* Trim gown with scatter lace and beads.
15. Sew snaps on back for closure.

Veiling: Refer to Pattern 41. Cut full circle nineteen inches in diameter and gather to fold at approximately seven inches from edge.

Illus. 151. Pattern 61 for bridal gown.

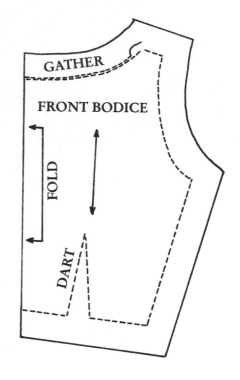

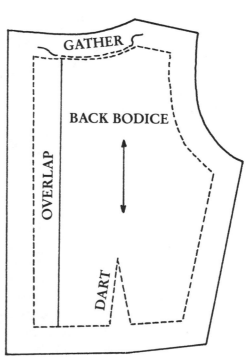

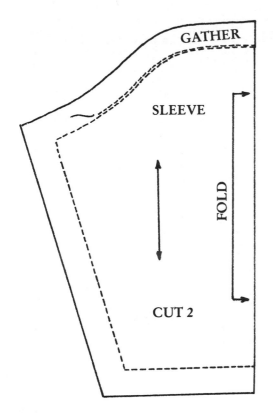

SLEEVE

FOLD

CUT 2

Illus. 151 (cont.).

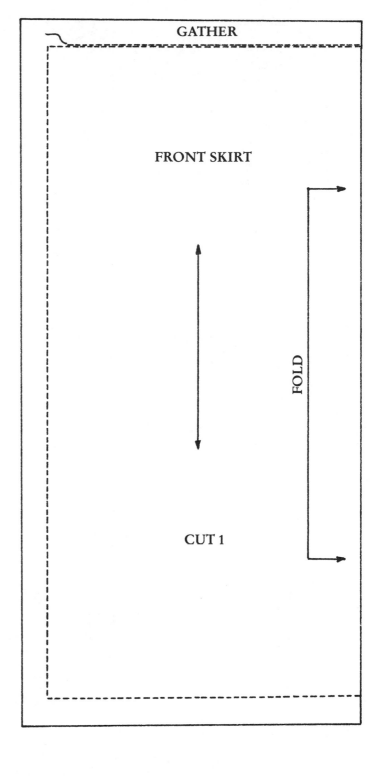

FRONT SKIRT

FOLD

CUT 1

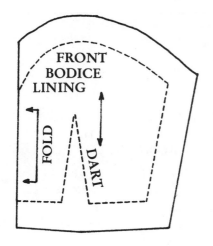

FRONT
BODICE
LINING

FOLD

DART

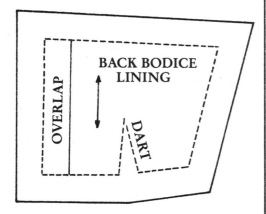

OVERLAP

BACK BODICE
LINING

DART

Illus. 151 (cont.).

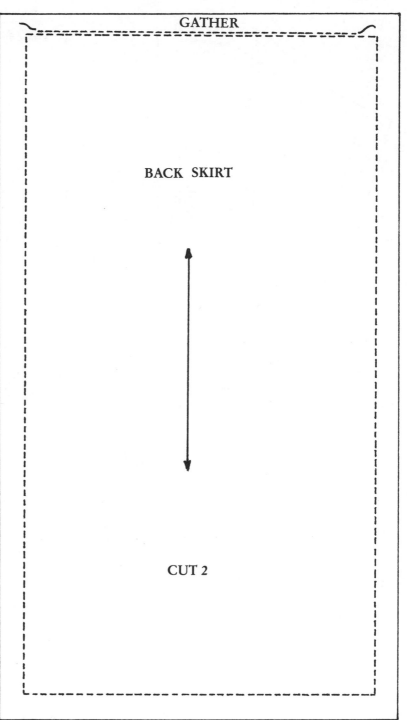

GATHER

BACK SKIRT

CUT 2

62. Gown

Illus. 152.   Front and back views of Pattern 62.

Supplies
Yardage based on 45″ width fabric.
⅓ yard lightweight dress fabric
6 small snaps
1 package assorted pearl beads (optional)
1 spool thread

PATTERN 62

This gown fits a twelve-inch fashion-type doll. Gown consists of ten parts and has a back opening.

Instructions

1. With right sides together, sew the darts of the front and back-bodice sections; set aside.
2. Gather the front-skirt and back-skirt panels.
3. With right sides together, sew the front bodice and front skirt together. Repeat the same procedure for the back sections.
4. With right sides together, sew the side seams of the gown.
5. Finish the raw edges of the bodice by turning under with stitching before sewing the shoulder straps.
6. Sew the shoulders straps to the gown.
7. Form ruffle by stitching through the center fold of the ruffle. Make sure that the raw edges are folded under to prevent from ravelling. When stringing ruffle, twist at intervals for a floral effect.
8. Finish the raw edges by turning under with stitching.
9. Sew snaps on back for closure.
10. Optional line for pearl beads.

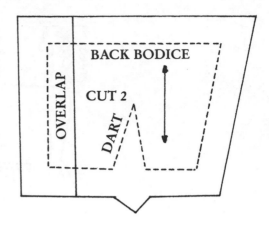

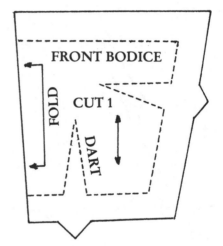

Illus. 153.   Pattern 62 for gown.

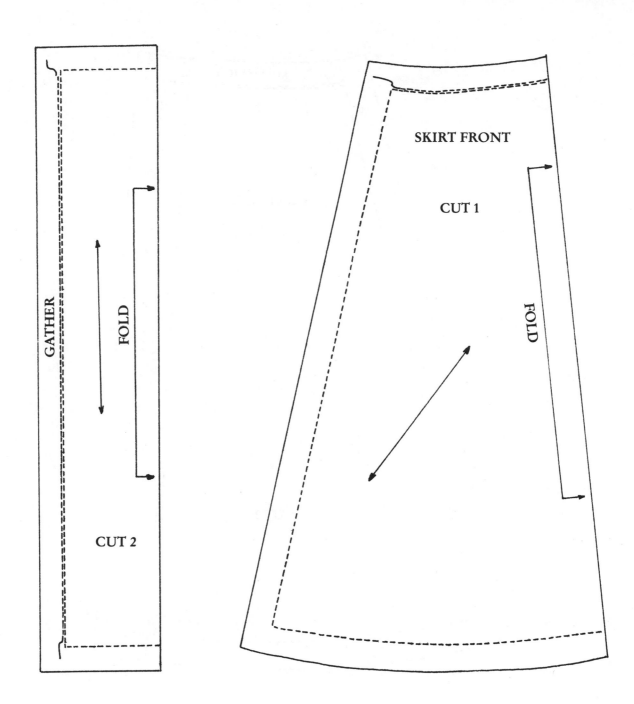

GATHER

FOLD

CUT 2

SKIRT FRONT

CUT 1

FOLD

Illus. 153 (cont.).

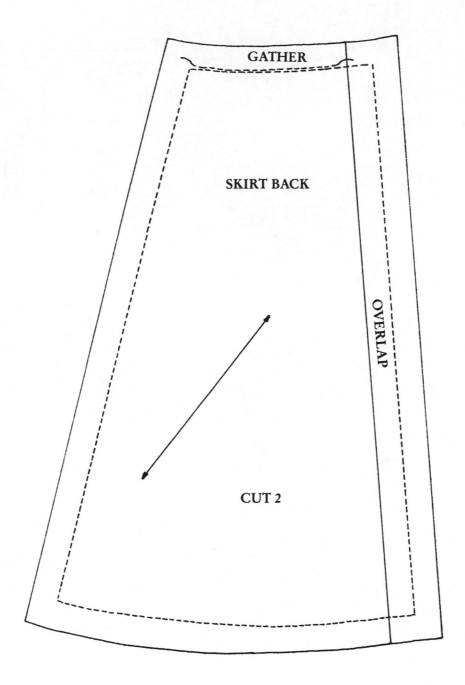

GATHER

SKIRT BACK

OVERLAP

CUT 2

Illus. 153 (cont.).

63. Shirt

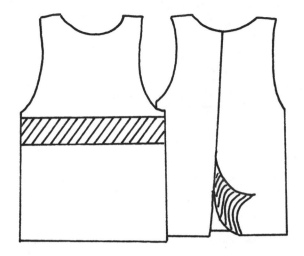

Illus. 154.   Front and back views of Pattern 63.

64. Shorts

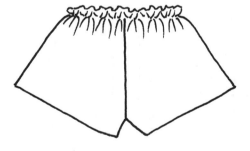

Illus. 155.   Front and back views of Pattern 64.

Supplies

Yardage estimates based on 45″ width fabric.

*⅛ yard lightweight knit fabric (combined yardage
    for Patterns 63 and 64)*

3½ inches ⅛″ wide elastic

1 spool thread

3 small snaps

PATTERN 63

This shirt fits a twelve-inch fashion-type doll. Shirt consists of three parts and has a back opening.

Instructions

1. With right sides together, sew the shoulder seams of the front bodice to the back bodice.

2. Turn under with stitching around the neckline and armholes of the shirt. Turning under with stitching at this stage of construction will greatly ease the finishing of the shirt. If desired, overlock or zigzag the edges.

3. With right sides together, sew the side seams of the shirt.

4. Turn under with stitching the hem and center-back sections of the shirt. If desired, use overlock or zigzag stitching.

5. Sew snaps on back for closure.

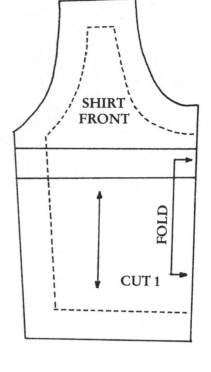

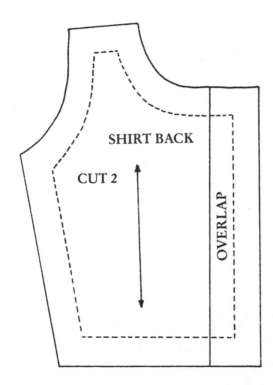

Illus. 156. Pattern 63 for shirt.

PATTERN 64

These shorts fit a twelve-inch fashion-type doll. Shorts consist of two parts and are elasticized at the waist.

Instructions

1. With right sides together, sew the crotch areas. (Refer to Illus. 16 on p. 9.)

2. Zigzag the edge of the pants and hemline.
3. At this point, attach elastic by machine.
4. With right sides together, sew the inner seams of the pants.

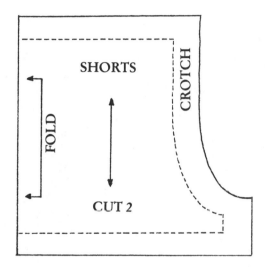

Illus. 157.   Pattern 64 for shorts.

65. Gown

Illus. 158.   Front and back views of Pattern 65.

Supplies
Yardage based on 45″ width fabric.
⅓ yard lightweight knit fabric
¼ yard ¼″ wide ribbon
1 spool thread
6 small snaps

PATTERN 65

This gown fits a twelve-inch fashion-type doll. The gown consists of four pattern pieces and has a back opening.

Instructions

1. Gather the shoulder of the front bodice to the width of the ribbon strap (about one-fourth inch).
2. Turn under with stitching all the raw edges of the front bodice.
3. With right sides together, sew the front panel of the skirt to the back panels, leaving the center of back unsewn.
4. With right sides together, sew the bodice to the skirt.
5. Sew ribbon ties from the shoulder seam (about four inches long, one-fourth inch wide). In addition, sew a ribbon tie to the center opposite side (right midsection) of the back bodice.
6. Finish the raw edges by turning under with stitching. For the inner raw edges, use zigzag or overlock stitching.
7. For closure, sew snaps on back.

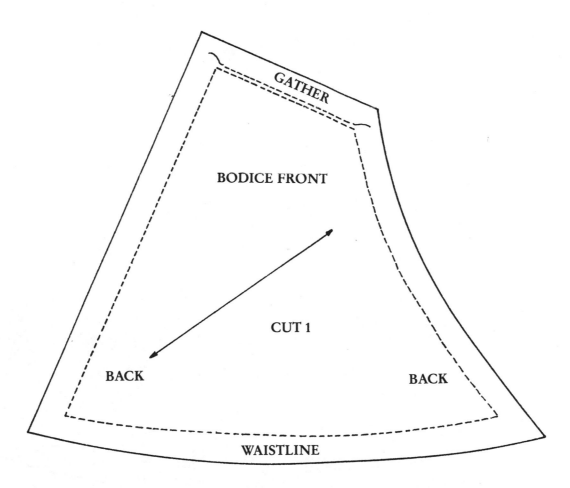

Illus. 159.   Pattern 65 for gown.

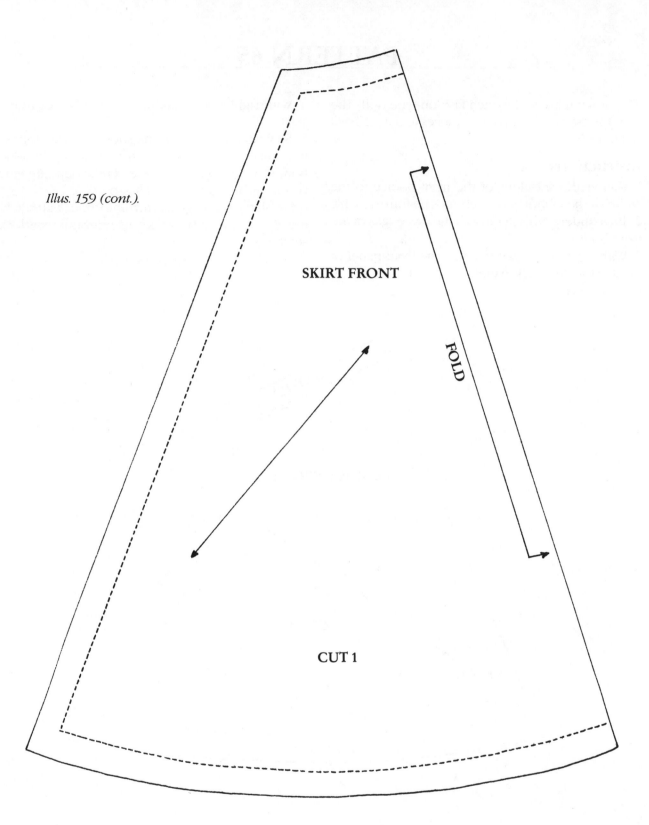

Illus. 159 (cont.).

SKIRT FRONT

FOLD

CUT 1

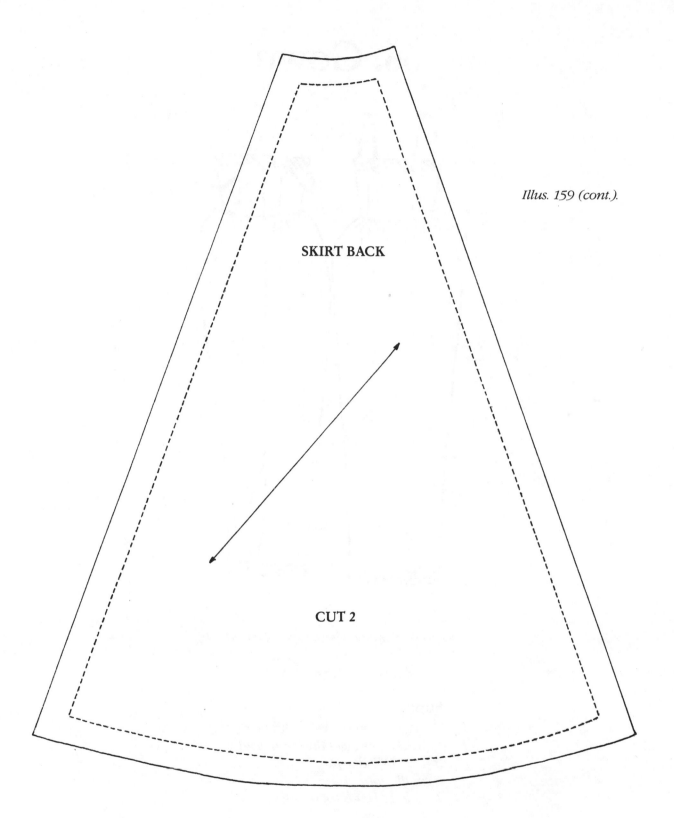

SKIRT BACK

CUT 2

66. Gown

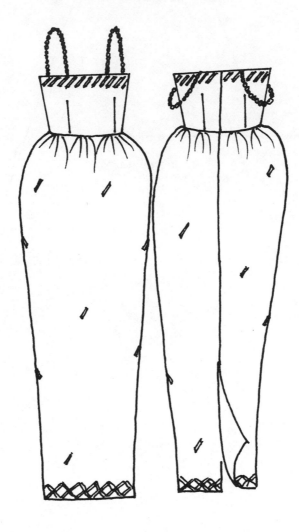

Illus. 160.   Front and back views of Pattern 66.

Supplies
Yardage based on 45″ width fabric.
¼ yard lightweight dress material
2″w × 15″l fake fur
6 small snaps
1 package beads (optional)
1 spool thread

PATTERN 66

This gown fits a twelve-inch fashion-type doll. Gown consists of six parts and has a back opening.

Instructions

1. With right sides together, sew the darts of the front and back bodice; set aside.
2. Gather the front- and back-skirt panels.
3. With right sides together, sew the front bodice to the front skirt. In the same way, sew the back-bodice sections to the respective skirt panels.
4. With right sides together, sew the side seams of the gown.
5. Finish the raw edges by turning under with stitching.
6. String beads about 2½″ in length for the shoulder straps.
7. Sew snaps on back of gown for closure.
8. *Optional:* Embellish the gown with contrasting beads.

Stole: Cut fake fur or real fur two inches wide and fifteen inches long. No sewing is required unless lining is desired.

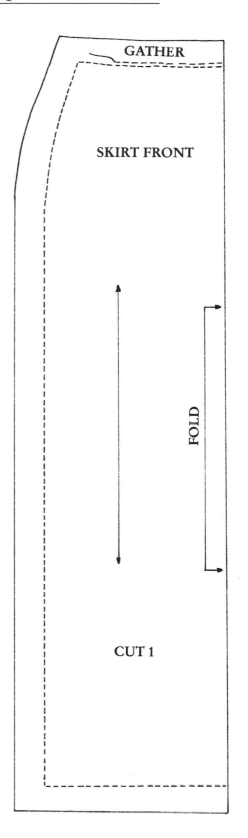

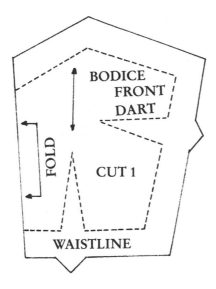

Illus. 161. Pattern 66 for gown.

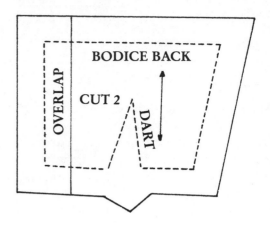

Illus. 161 (cont.).

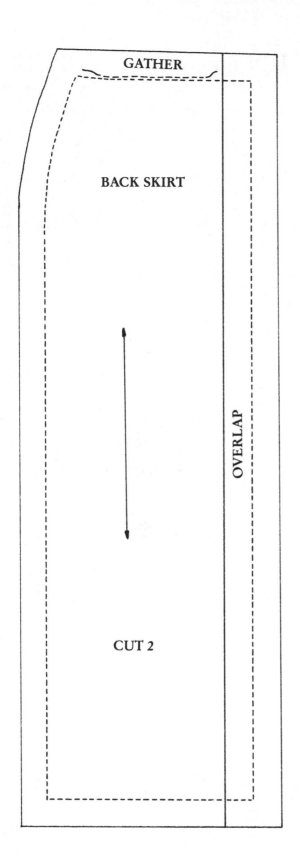

67. Gown

68. Pinafore

Illus. 162. Front and back views of Patterns 67 and 68.

Supplies
Yardage based on 45" width fabric.
½ yard dress fabric (Pattern 67 only)
¼ yard lace or dress fabric
1 spool thread
12 small snaps
1½ yards ¼" wide lace trim (optional)
1 yard ¼" ribbon

PATTERN 67

This gown fits a fifteen-inch baby-type doll. Gown consists of ten parts. Front skirt consists of three panels plus two panels for the back skirt. Gown has back opening.

Instructions

1. With right sides together, sew the shoulder seam of the front bodice to the back-bodice sections. Set aside.
2. Gather the sleeves.
3. At this point, hem the sleeves. *Optional:* For elasticized sleeves, proceed to attach elastic to the cuffs of the sleeves.
4. With right sides together, sew the sleeves to the bodice; set aside.
5. With right sides together, join three skirt panels to form the front skirt.
6. Gather the front skirt. In the same way, gather the two back-skirt panels.
7. With right sides together, sew the front skirt to the front bodice of the gown. Repeat this step for the back sections.
8. With right sides together, sew the side seams of the gown starting from the hem of the sleeves to the hem of the gown.
9. Finish the raw edges by turning under with stitching.
10. For closure, sew snaps on back of gown.

Illus. 163.   Pattern 67 for gown.

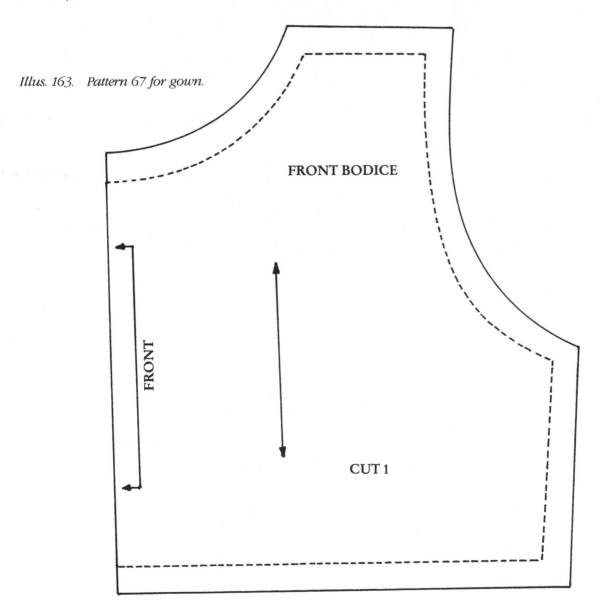

FRONT BODICE

FRONT

CUT 1

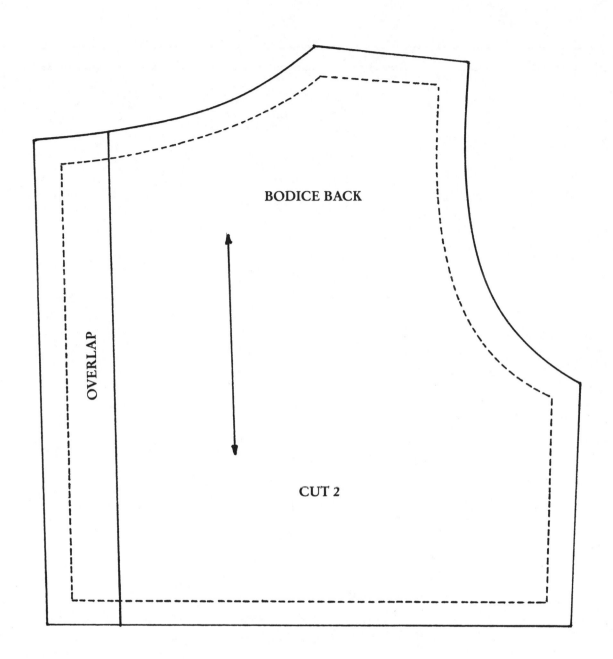

Illus. 163 (cont.).

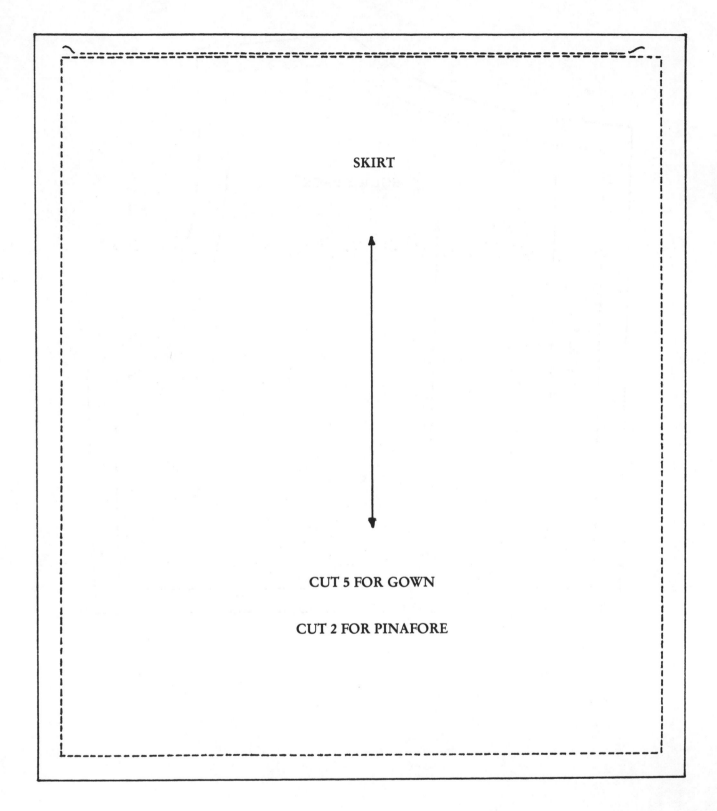

SKIRT

CUT 5 FOR GOWN

CUT 2 FOR PINAFORE

Illus. 163 (cont.).

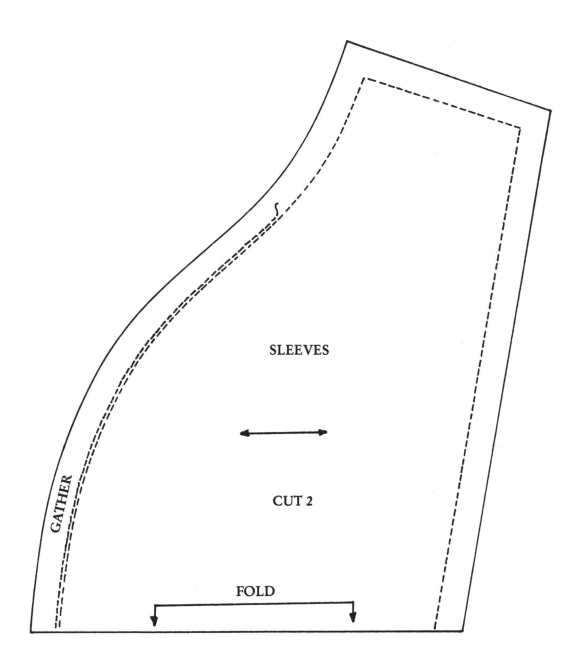

SLEEVES

GATHER

CUT 2

FOLD

Illus. 163 (cont.).

PATTERN 68

This pinafore fits a fifteen-inch baby-type doll. Pinafore consists of six parts. Pinafore opens in back and is tied at the sides. Use skirt pattern 67 for the two back-skirt panels required.

Instructions

1. Finish the skirt edges of the front- and back-skirt panels (edges to be gathered) by turning under with stitching.
2. Gather the front-skirt and back-skirt panels.
3. With right sides together, sew the bodice front to the front skirt. Repeat this step for the back sections.
4. With right sides together, sew the shoulder seams of the front bodice to the back-bodice sections.
5. Finish the raw edges by turning under with stitching.
6. Sew ribbon ties to the sides of the pinafore.
7. *Optional:* Embellish pinafore with scattered lace and lace strips for a dressy effect.

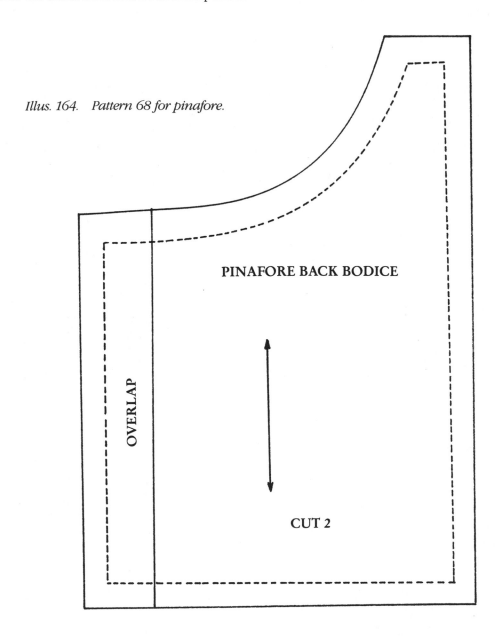

Illus. 164.   Pattern 68 for pinafore.

PINAFORE BACK BODICE

OVERLAP

CUT 2

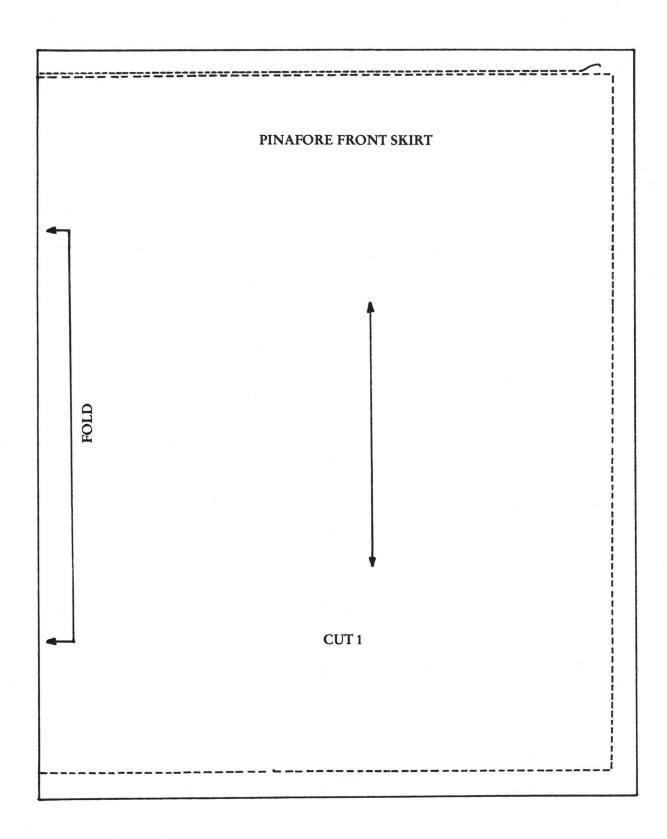

Illus. 164 (cont.).

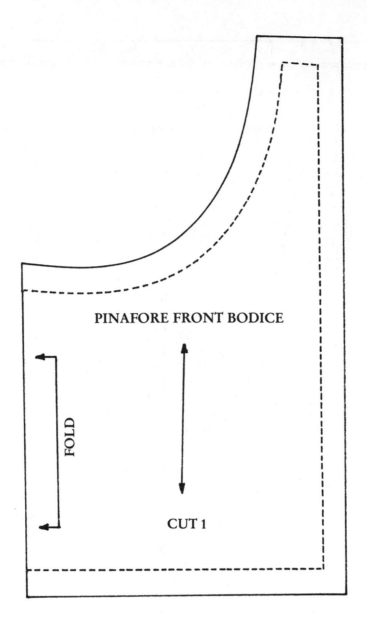

PINAFORE FRONT BODICE

FOLD

CUT 1

Illus. 164 (cont.).

69. Party Dress

Illus. 165.   Front and back views of Pattern 69.

Supplies
Yardage based on 45″ width fabric.
⅓ yard lightweight satin fabric
¾ yard 1″ wide lace trim (optional for sleeves)
⅔ yard ¼″ wide lace trim (optional for bodice)
5 small snaps
1 spool thread

This party dress fits a fifteen-inch baby-type doll. Dress consists of nine parts. To avoid a seam line on the front of the skirt, the skirt may be divided into three parts instead of four: one panel for the front skirt and two panels for the back. The skirt can also be cut in one continuous piece. Dress has a back opening.

Instructions

1. With right sides together, sew two skirt panels to form the front skirt.

2. Gather sleeves, the front skirt and the back-skirt panels.

3. With right sides together, sew the front bodice to the front skirt. Repeat this step for the back sections.

4. With right sides together, sew the shoulder seams of the front bodice to the back-bodice sections.

5. At this point, hem the sleeves by turning under with stitching.

6. With right sides together, sew the sleeves to the bodice.

7. With right sides together, sew the side seams of the dress starting at the hem of the sleeves to the hem of the dress.

8. Finish the raw edges by turning under with stitching.

9. *Optional:* Trim dress with lace.

10. Sew snaps on back for closure.

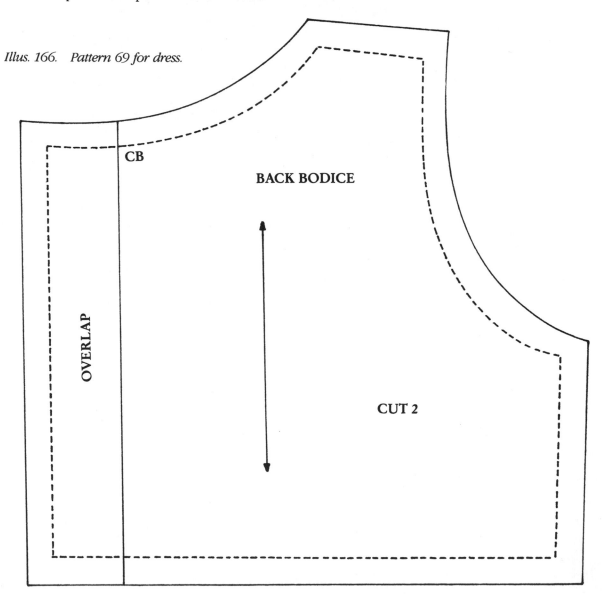

Illus. 166. Pattern 69 for dress.

CB

BACK BODICE

OVERLAP

CUT 2

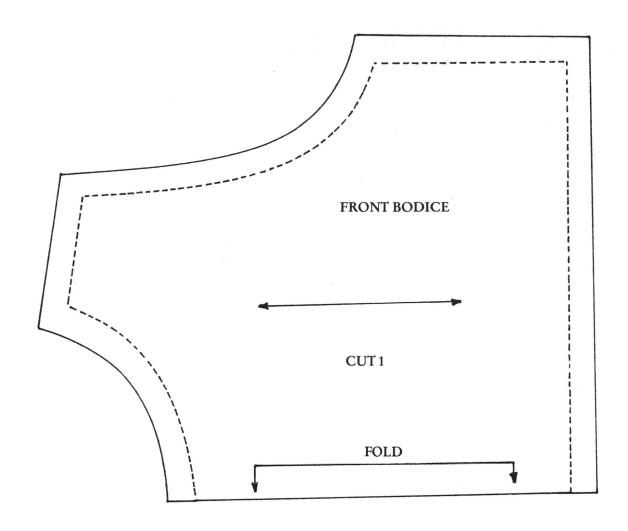

FRONT BODICE

CUT 1

FOLD

Illus. 166 (cont.).

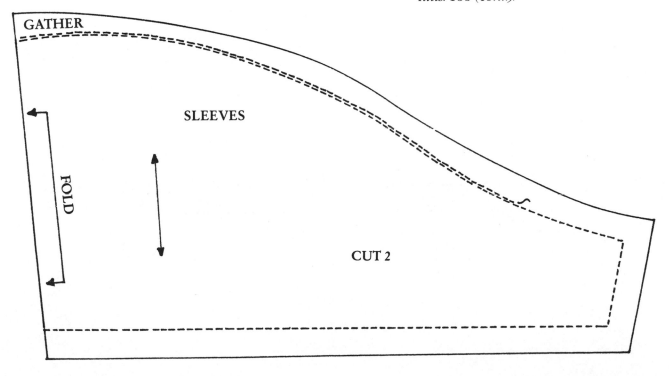

GATHER

SLEEVES

FOLD

CUT 2

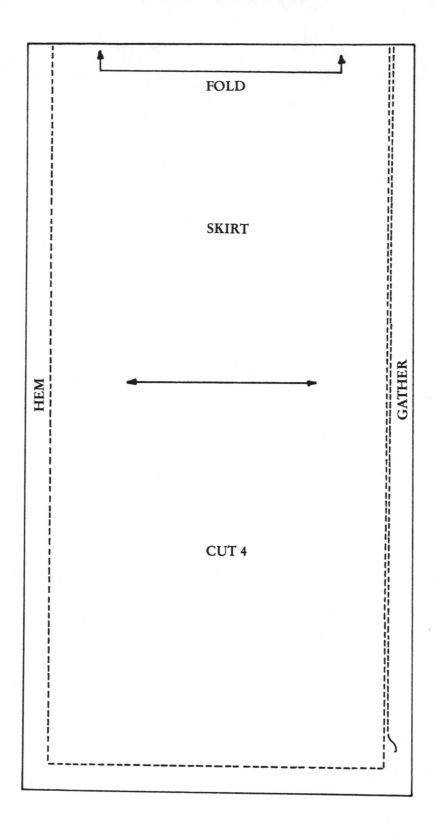

FOLD

SKIRT

HEM

GATHER

CUT 4

Illus. 166 (cont.).

70. Nightgown

Illus. 167.   Front and back views of Pattern 70.

Supplies

Yardage based on 45" width fabric.
½ yard flannel or fleece fabric
1⅓ yards ½" wide gathered trimming lace
(optional)
24 inches single-fold bias tape (optional)
1 spool thread
6 small snaps

This nightgown fits a fifteen-inch baby-type doll. Nightgown consists of ten parts and has a back opening and elasticized sleeves.

Instructions

1. With right sides together, sew the front yoke to the back-yoke sections; set aside.

2. At this point, attach lace and elastic to the sleeves.

3. With right sides together, sew the sleeves to the bodice of the nightgown.

4. Gather the bodice to fit the yoke of the nightgown.

5. With right sides together, sew the yoke to the bodice of the nightgown.

6. With right sides together, sew the side seams of the gown starting at the hem of the sleeves to the hem of the nightgown.

7. Finish the pockets by turning under with stitching.

8. Position the pockets and topstitch in place.

9. Finish the neckline with a bias tape or by turning under with stitching.

10. Finish the remaining raw edges by turning under with stitching.

11. *Optional:* Trim the gown with lace.

12. For closure, sew snaps on back of nightgown.

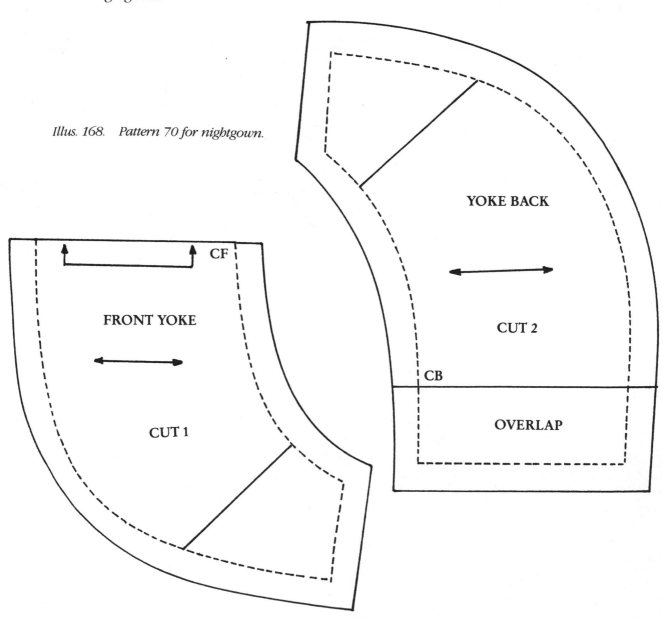

Illus. 168.   Pattern 70 for nightgown.

FRONT YOKE

CF

CUT 1

YOKE BACK

CUT 2

CB

OVERLAP

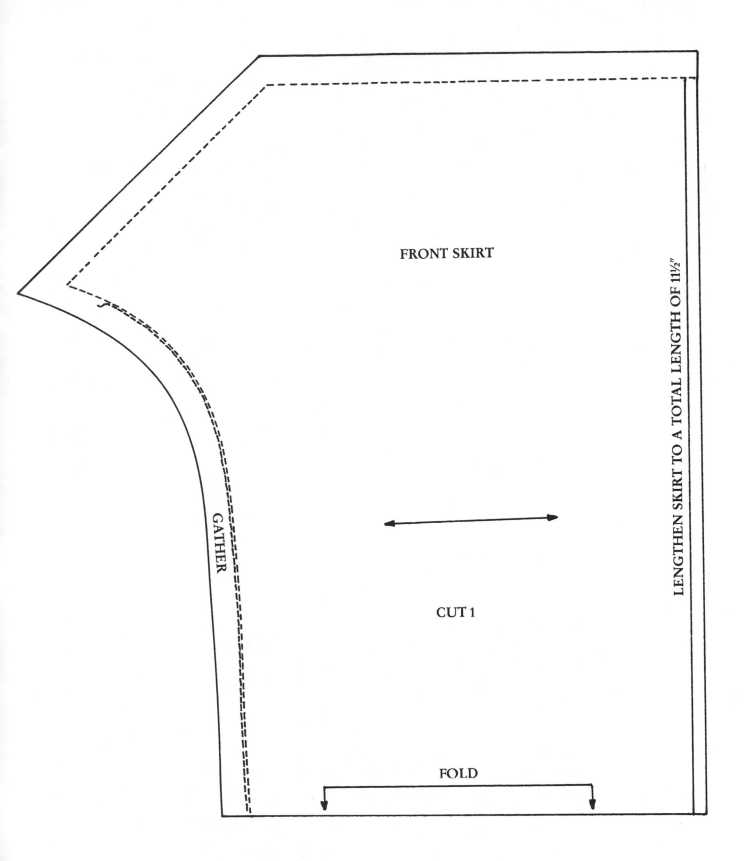

FRONT SKIRT

GATHER

CUT 1

FOLD

LENGTHEN SKIRT TO A TOTAL LENGTH OF 11½"

Illus. 168 (cont.).

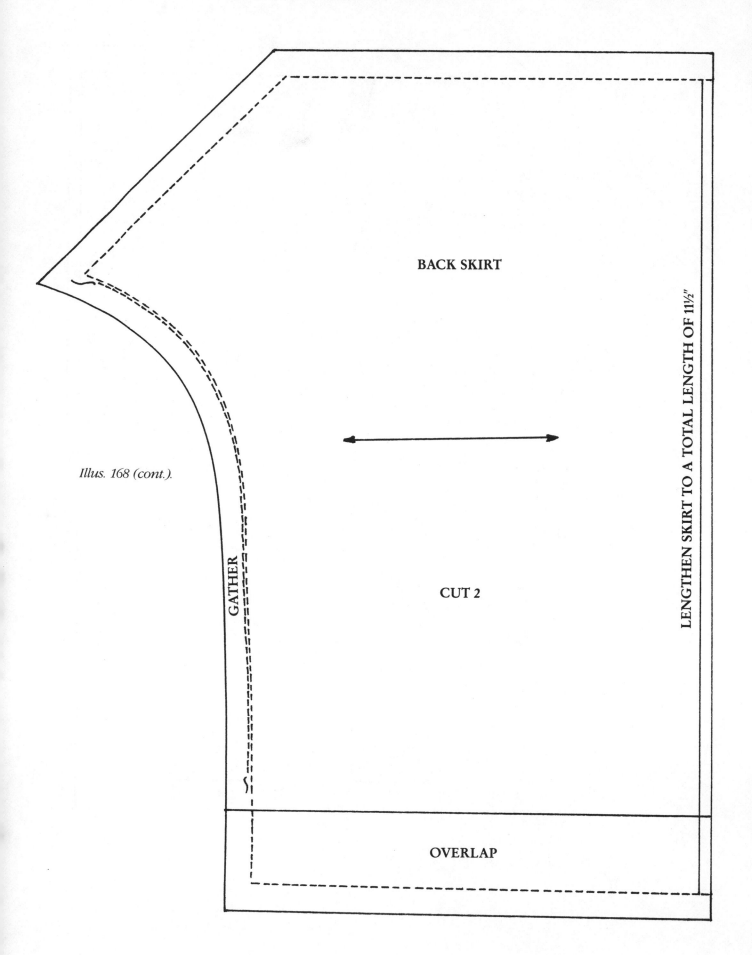

BACK SKIRT

LENGTHEN SKIRT TO A TOTAL LENGTH OF 11½"

Illus. 168 (cont.).

GATHER

CUT 2

OVERLAP

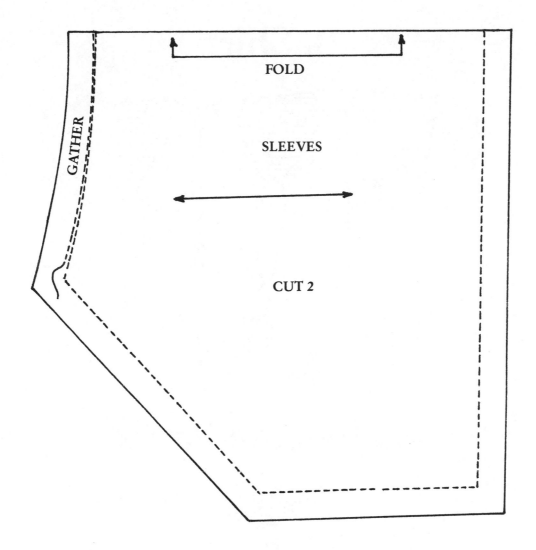

Illus. 168 (cont.).

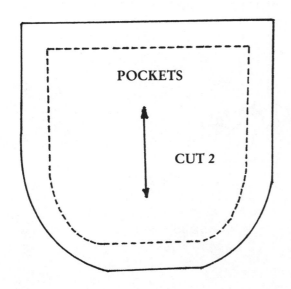

71. Shirt

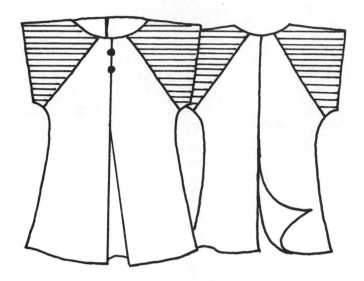

Illus. 169.   Front and back views of Pattern 71.

72. Jogging Pants

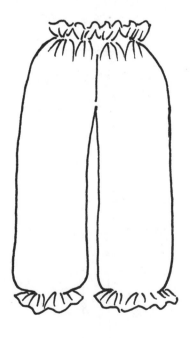

Illus. 170.   Front and back views of Pattern 72.

Supplies

Yardage based on 45″ width fabric.

⅓ *yard lightweight knit fabric (combined yardage for Patterns 71 and 72)*

2 small 4-hole buttons (optional)

1 spool thread

1 yard ¼″ width elastic

5″l × 20″w lightweight knit fabric (optional for contrasting sleeves)

3 small snaps

PATTERN 71

This shirt fits a fifteen-inch baby-type doll. Shirt consists of five parts and has a back opening.

Instructions

1. With right sides together, stitch the pleat of the shirt. Press the pleats in place.
2. With right sides together, sew the sleeves to the bodice of the shirt.
3. At this point, hem the sleeves by turning under with stitching.
4. With right sides together, sew the side seams of the shirt.
5. Finish the raw edges by turning under with stitching.
6. Sew snaps on back for closure.

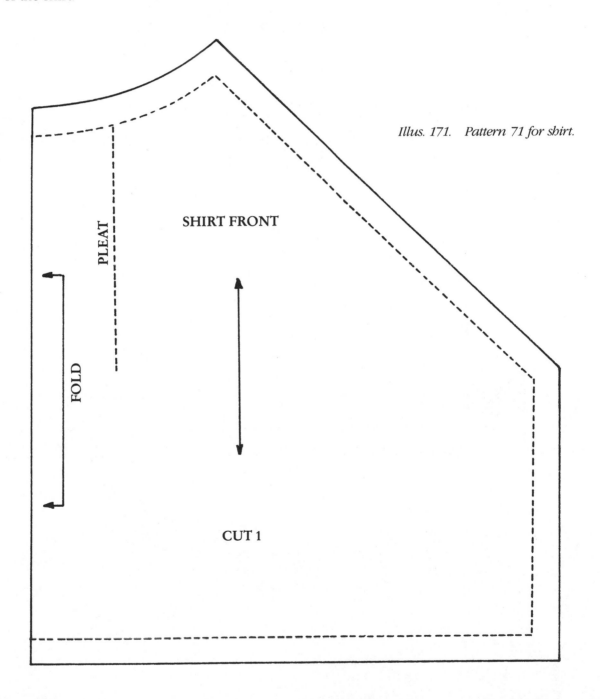

Illus. 171. Pattern 71 for shirt.

PLEAT

SHIRT FRONT

FOLD

CUT 1

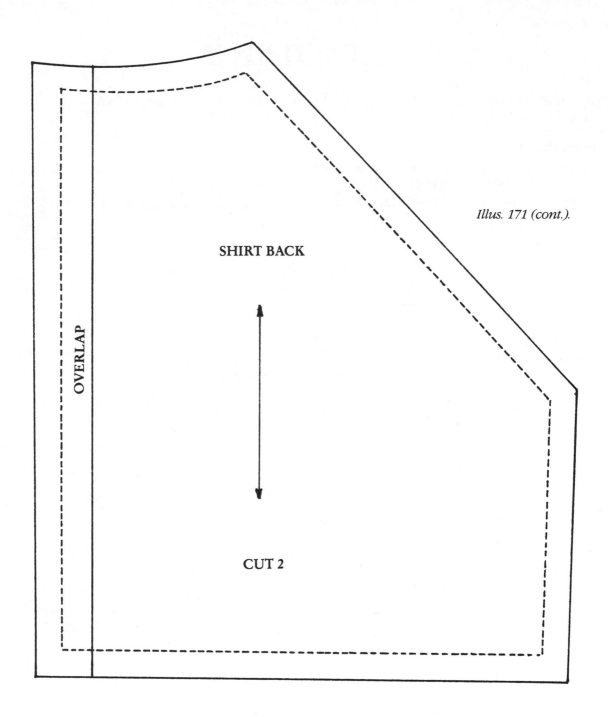

SHIRT BACK

OVERLAP

CUT 2

Illus. 171 (cont.).

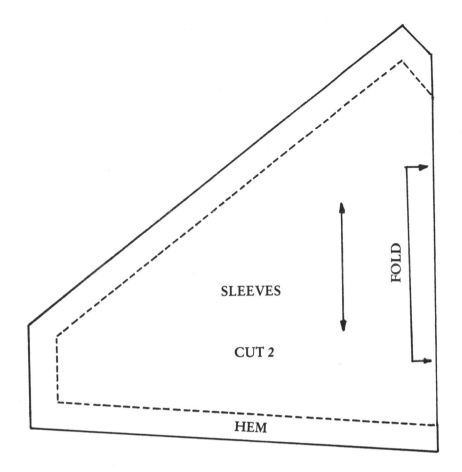

SLEEVES

CUT 2

FOLD

HEM

Illus. 171 (cont.).

PATTERN 72

These jogging pants fit a fifteen-inch baby-type doll. Jogging pants consist of two parts only and are elasticized at the waist and ankles.

Instructions

1. With right sides together, sew the crotch sections of the jogging pants. Refer to Illus. 16 and 17.
2. Finish the raw edges of the waist and hem of pants with zigzag or overlock stitching.

3. At this point, attach the elastic to the hem of the pants.
4. With right sides together, sew the inseam of the pants.
5. Attach elastic to the waist of the jogging pants.

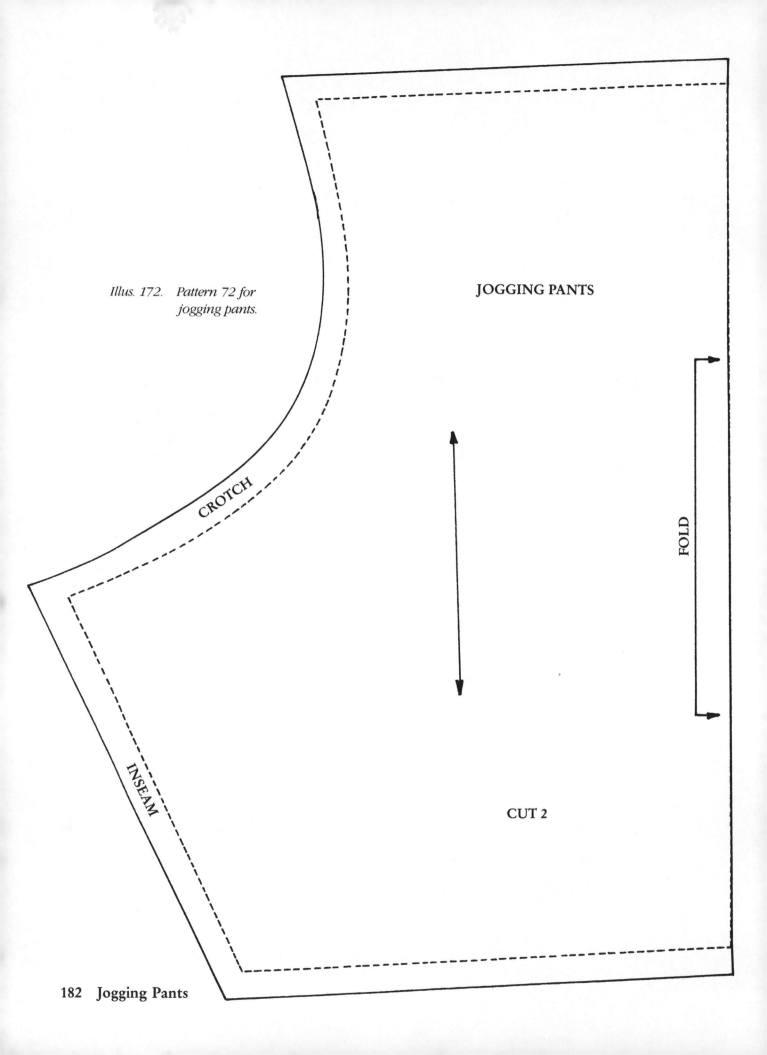

Illus. 172. Pattern 72 for jogging pants.

JOGGING PANTS

CROTCH

FOLD

INSEAM

CUT 2

73. Dress

Illus. 173.   Front and back views of Pattern 73.

Supplies
Yardage based on 45″ width fabric.
⅓ yard lightweight dress fabric
4 small snaps
1 spool thread
1½ yards ¼″ wide trimming lace (optional)

PATTERN 73

This dress fits a fifteen-inch baby-type doll. Dress consists of five parts and has a back opening.

Instructions

1. With right sides together, sew the pleat of the front bodice. Press pleat in place.
2. With right sides together, sew the shoulder seams of the dress.
3. Gather the sleeves.
4. At this point, finish the hem of the sleeves by turning under with stitching.
5. With right sides together, sew the sleeves to the bodice.
6. With right sides together, sew the side seams of the dress.
7. Finish the remaining raw edges by turning under with stitching.
8. Finish the edges of the pockets by turning under with stitching.
9. Position pockets and topstitch in place.
10. *Optional:* Trim dress with lace.
11. For closure, sew snaps on back of dress.

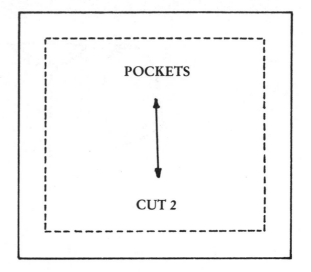

Illus. 174. Pattern 73 for dress.

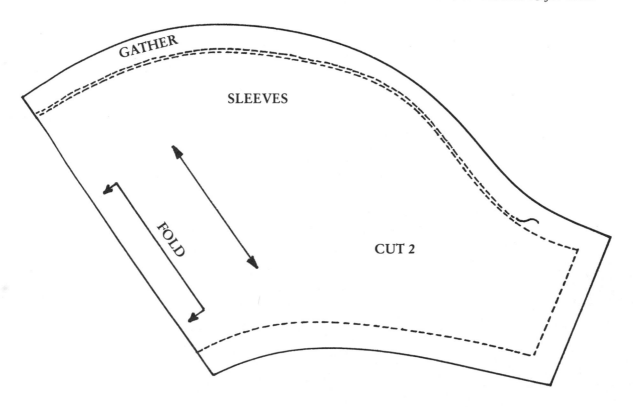

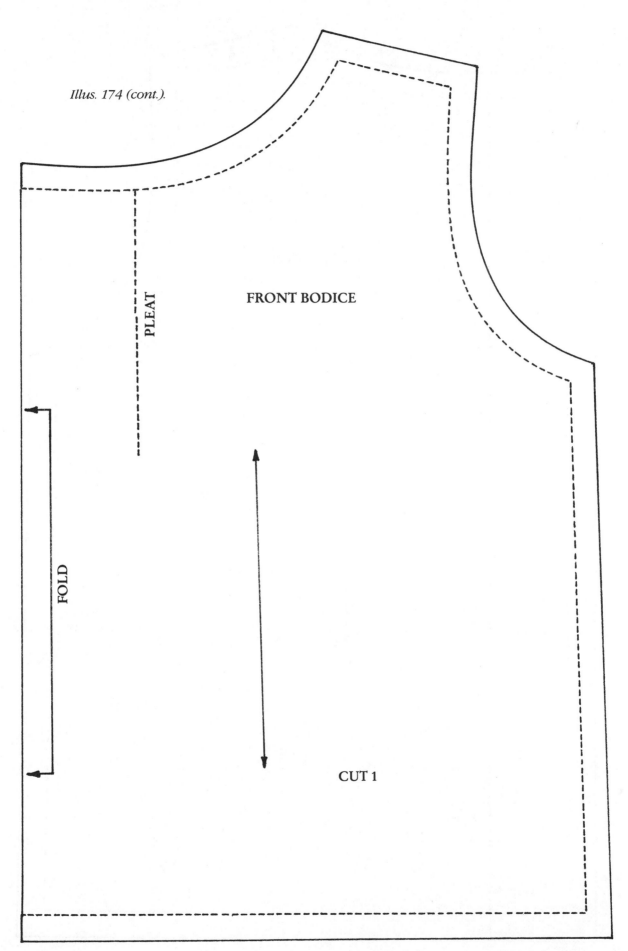

Illus. 174 (cont.).

PLEAT

FRONT BODICE

FOLD

CUT 1

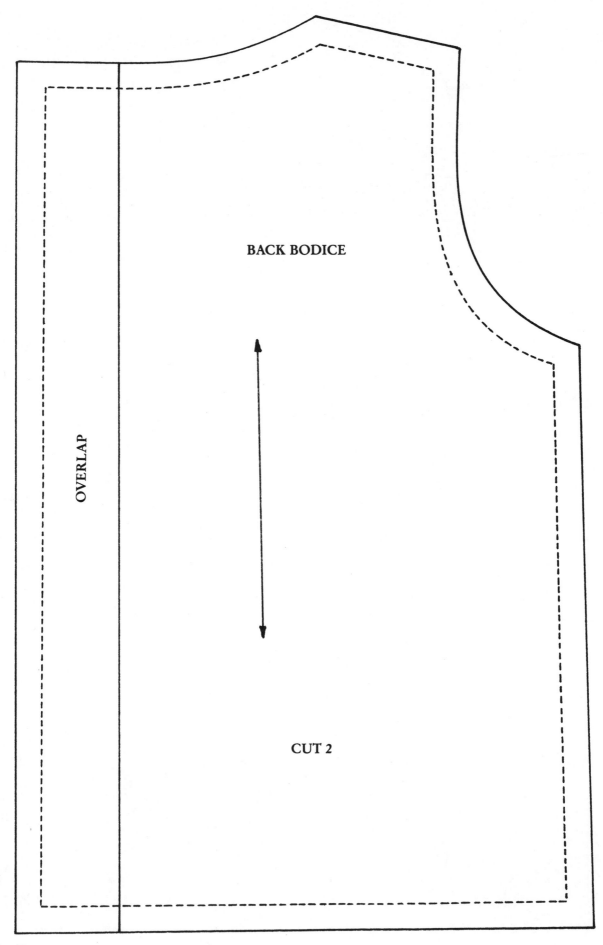

BACK BODICE

OVERLAP

CUT 2

HISTORY OF THE DOLL

he origins of the doll have been traced back by historians to religious rites of primitive societies. Historians further speculate that as beliefs faded, the importance of the doll waned. As a result, the dolls were handed down to children as toys. Evidence of the link between the doll and religious rites is supported by ancient Greek literature, in which girls were observed making clothing for their dolls and offering these valued playthings to the nymphs or to Artemis at the time of their engagement for marriage. Further evidence was noted by Boehn, an historian, on the practice of the Hopi Indians who, at the conclusion of ceremonial rites, gave the dolls to the children to play with.

The earliest samples of European dolls dated from the fourteenth century in Nuremberg, Germany. These dolls were modelled after children, monks and women and dressed in the fashion of the time. One notable characteristic of these dolls was a circular hollow in the breast. It has been speculated that these cavities may have been designed to hold a christening gift, such as a florin. Archeologists noted the existence of similar dolls in diggings, which indicated that these dolls were made in multiple numbers. These discoveries indicated that the doll industry was a thriving enterprise at this time.

Listings of dollmaker names in the city records of Nuremberg were dated as early as the fifteenth century. During this period, guilds of dollmakers were also established in the city, which regulated the types of dolls made and the methods of distribution of these dolls by peddlers.

An actual specimen of a doll made in the 1500's was found in 1966 in a Rhenish castle, giving us a glimpse of the period dolls of this time. This nine-inch doll was described by Hillier, an historian, as one carved in limewood and embellished with colored paint. The doll wore a tightly bodiced linen dress, which extended to the neckline, held in place with gold embroidery. A matching embroidered wide stomacher was worn over the girdle of the dress. The doll wore a net cap, with rounded points, which was drawn down to the side, over her ears. It can be noted that dolls dated in the 1500's bear testimony to the costume period when compared to the paintings of this time.

Fashion dolls became popular around the 1300's. Court records noted events such as the gifts of fashion dolls sent by the French queen to the queen of England in 1321. Another event that was noted was when Isabeau of Bavaria, queen of France, sent dolls to England from France to show the newest French fashions in 1391. In essence, the task of popularizing French fashions abroad was carried on by the doll.

To far-reaching colonies, such as North America, Parisian dolls were sent to illustrate the current Parisian fashions and to serve as the dressmaker's model as well. An advertisement of the *New England Weekly Journal* of July 2, 1733 read as follows:

At Mrs. Hannah Teatt's, dressmaker at the top of Summer Street, Boston, is to be seen a mannequin, in the latest fashion, with articles of dress, night dresses, and everything appertaining to women's attire. It has been brought from London by Captain White. Ladies who choose to see it may come or send for it. It is always ready to serve you. If you come, it will cost you two shillings, but if you send for it, seven shillings.

It can be noted that these fashion dolls were exempted from embargoes even at the time of wars during the 1300's to the 1800's.

The practice of sending costume dolls to other countries remained popular until the emergence of the hand-colored fashion plates. Fashion magazines such as *The Lady's Magazine, Entertaining Companion for the Fair Sex, Polite Depository of Amusement and Instruction, The Lady's Monthly Museum,* and *Instruct the Mind and Exalt the Character of the British Fair* all enjoyed popularity late in the 1700's. These magazines became the major source of fashion information for the ladies of the time. The magazines gradually replaced the fashion dolls as the means of fashion communication between countries.

The Doll Industry in Europe

Germany as the leading doll manufacturer in Europe during the nineteenth and the early part of the twentieth century dominated the doll market in Europe and abroad. It has been estimated that about seventy-five percent of these German dolls were sold in the British Isles and the United States. Germany became the leading doll manufacturer for two reasons. One reason was the abundance of raw materials such as wood. Another was the need of its agricultural society for occupation during the long winter months. Although dolls were cast from the same or similar moulds, doll characteristics varied from dollmaker to dollmaker.

Dollmakers in Germany were grouped in two regions: the Saxon Ore Mountains where papier-mâché, wood, and leather toys were made, and Nuremberg and Sonneberg where wood and metal toys were produced. On a smaller scale, France, Austria and England also engaged in the blossoming doll industry.

The Doll Industry in the United States

Prior to World War I, the United States imported dolls from Germany, Austria, France, England and Japan. World War I generated the building of the American doll industry due to embargoes on goods, especially those of German origin. The incentive of the doll market's profitability induced many smaller companies to engage only in the sale of dolls, such as the E. I. Horsman Doll, Incorporated.

Materials of all types were employed in the production of the American doll. Composition limbs and heads, made of glue and sawdust, were commonly utilized along with leather for the toy's body. Wooden dolls were manufactured in smaller scale by fewer companies.

Originally developed for military use, in 1948, the use of plastics became popular. With this advent, hard plastic dolls replaced other types of dolls in the consumer market. The vinyl plastic doll was later introduced, which is still utilized by the doll industry as we know it today.

METRIC EQUIVALENCY CHART

MM—MILLIMETRES   CM—CENTIMETRES

INCHES TO MILLIMETRES AND CENTIMETRES

INCHES	MM	CM	INCHES	CM	INCHES	CM
⅛	3	0.3	9	22.9	30	76.2
¼	6	0.6	10	25.4	31	78.7
⅜	10	1.0	11	27.9	32	81.3
½	13	1.3	12	30.5	33	83.8
⅝	16	1.6	13	33.0	34	86.4
¾	19	1.9	14	35.6	35	88.9
⅞	22	2.2	15	38.1	36	91.4
1	25	2.5	16	40.6	37	94.0
1¼	32	3.2	17	43.2	38	96.5
1½	38	3.8	18	45.7	39	99.1
1¾	44	4.4	19	48.3	40	101.6
2	51	5.1	20	50.8	41	104.1
2½	64	6.4	21	53.3	42	106.7
3	76	7.6	22	55.9	43	109.2
3½	89	8.9	23	58.4	44	111.8
4	102	10.2	24	61.0	45	114.3
4½	114	11.4	25	63.5	46	116.8
5	127	12.7	26	66.0	47	119.4
6	152	15.2	27	68.6	48	121.9
7	178	17.8	28	71.1	49	124.5
8	203	20.3	29	73.7	50	127.0

YARDS TO METRES

YARDS	METRES	YARDS	METRES	YARDS	METRES	YARDS	METRES	YARDS	METRES
⅛	0.11	2⅛	1.94	4⅛	3.77	6⅛	5.60	8⅛	7.43
¼	0.23	2¼	2.06	4¼	3.89	6¼	5.72	8¼	7.54
⅜	0.34	2⅜	2.17	4⅜	4.00	6⅜	5.83	8⅜	7.66
½	0.46	2½	2.29	4½	4.11	6½	5.94	8½	7.77
⅝	0.57	2⅝	2.40	4⅝	4.23	6⅝	6.06	8⅝	7.89
¾	0.69	2¾	2.51	4¾	4.34	6¾	6.17	8¾	8.00
⅞	0.80	2⅞	2.63	4⅞	4.46	6⅞	6.29	8⅞	8.12
1	0.91	3	2.74	5	4.57	7	6.40	9	8.23
1⅛	1.03	3⅛	2.86	5⅛	4.69	7⅛	6.52	9⅛	8.34
1¼	1.14	3¼	2.97	5¼	4.80	7¼	6.63	9¼	8.46
1⅜	1.26	3⅜	3.09	5⅜	4.91	7⅜	6.74	9⅜	8.57
1½	1.37	3½	3.20	5½	5.03	7½	6.86	9½	8.69
1⅝	1.49	3⅝	3.31	5⅝	5.14	7⅝	6.97	9⅝	8.80
1¾	1.60	3¾	3.43	5¾	5.26	7¾	7.09	9¾	8.92
1⅞	1.71	3⅞	3.54	5⅞	5.37	7⅞	7.20	9⅞	9.03
2	1.83	4	3.66	6	5.49	8	7.32	10	9.14

INDEX

ABOUT THE AUTHOR

Roselyn Gadia-Smitley is a graduate of California State University, Los Angeles, with a master of arts and bachelor of arts in Textiles and Clothing. Her area of study has been primarily in textiles, clothing construction, interiors, art, fashion design and fashion merchandising.

The author's work experience included two and a half years of college instruction in fashion design, merchandising and crafts. She also holds a lifetime teaching credential for community colleges in the state of California.

The author is a doll collector and a self-taught porcelain dollmaker. Her other interests include quilting, lacemaking, crochet, knitting, fabric painting, batik, smocking, weaving, ceramics and photography.